COOKSHELF
Chocolate

Jacqueline Bellefontaine

p

This is a Parragon Publishing Book
This edition published in 2005

Parragon Publishing
Queen Street House
4 Queen Street
Bath BA1 1HE, UK

ISBN: 0-75255-526-X

Printed in China

Note

Cup measurements in this book are for American cups. Tablespoons are
assumed to be 15 ml. Unless otherwise stated, milk is assumed to be full fat,
eggs are medium and pepper is freshly ground black pepper.

The equipment on pages 20-21, 30-31, 40-41, 68-69, 90-91, 156-157 and 212-213
was kindly supplied by Divertimenti, 139 Fulham Rd, London SW3

Contents

Introduction

Chocolate is one of life's luxuries and one of the few that we can all afford. This book contains all the recipes you need to enjoy this luxury at any time of the day. For example, you could wake up to Pain au Chocolat with your morning coffee. You could indulge in a hot chocolate dessert at lunchtime, have a sumptuous slice of chocolate cake as an afternoon snack, luxuriate with a rich chocolate dessert as part of the evening meal, and round off the end of the day with a comforting hot chocolate. While this might seem to be taking things too far, even for the most hardened chocoholic, why not tempt yourself with a perfect chocolate treat now and then? Go on, spoil yourself!

Chocolate is produced from the beans of the cacao tree, which originated in South America, but now grows in Africa, the West Indies, the tropical parts of the United States, and the Far East. Cacao beans are large pods – once harvested, both the pulp from the pods and the bean are allowed to ferment in the sun. The pulp evaporates and the bean develops its chocolaty flavor. The outer skin is then removed and the beans are left in the sun for a little longer or roasted. Finally, they are shelled and the kernels are used for making cocoa and chocolate.

The kernels have to be ground and processed to produce a thick mixture or paste called "cocoa solids" and it is this that we refer to when gauging the quality of chocolate. The cocoa solids are then pressed to remove some of the fat – "cocoa butter." They are then further processed to produce the product that we know and love as chocolate.

STORING CHOCOLATE

Store chocolate in a cool, dry place away from direct heat or sunlight. Most chocolate can be stored for about one year. It can be stored in the refrigerator, but make sure it is well wrapped, as it will pick up flavors from other foods. Chocolate decorations can be stored in airtight containers and interleaved with nonstick baking parchment. Dark chocolate will keep for four weeks, and milk and white chocolate for two.

MELTING CHOCOLATE

Chocolate should not be melted over direct heat, except when melted with other ingredients, and even then, the heat should be very low.

Break the chocolate into small, equal-size pieces and place them in the top pan of a double boiler. Heat the water in the bottom pan. (If you don't have a double boiler, use a heatproof bowl placed over a pan of hot water.) Make sure the base is not in contact with the water. Once the chocolate starts to melt, stir gently, and, if necessary, leave over the water a little longer. No drops of water or steam should come into contact with the melted chocolate, as it will solidify.

To melt chocolate in the microwave, break the chocolate into small pieces and place in a microwave-safe bowl. Timing will vary according to the type and quantity of chocolate. As a guide, melt 4$\frac{1}{2}$ ounces dark chocolate on high for 2 minutes, and white or milk chocolate for 2–3 minutes on Medium. Stir the chocolate and let stand for a few minutes, then stir again. Return to the microwave for a further 30 seconds if necessary.

SETTING CHOCOLATE

Chocolate sets best at 65°F, although it will set (more slowly) in a slightly warmer room. If possible set chocolate for decorations in a cool room. If set in the refrigerator it may develop a white bloom.

TYPES OF CHOCOLATE

Dark Chocolate *can contain anything from 30 to 75 per cent cocoa solids. It has a slightly sweet flavor and a dark color. It is the chocolate most used in cooking. For everyday cooking and the majority of these recipes calling for dark chocolate, choose one with around 50 percent cocoa solids. However, dark chocolate with a higher cocoa solid content will give a richer, more intense flavor. This chocolate is often called luxury or continental chocolate and has a cocoa solid content of between 70-75 per cent. Occasionally it is essential to use a better chocolate and I have indicated in the individual recipes where this is the case.*

Milk Chocolate, *as its name suggests, contains milk and has a lovely creamy, mild and sweet flavor. It is mostly used as an eating chocolate, rather than in cooking. However it does have its place in chocolate cooking, especially for decorations and when a milder, creamy flavor is required. It is more sensitive to heat than dark chocolate so care must be taken when melting it.*

White Chocolate *contains a lower cocoa butter content and cocoa solids. It can be quite temperamental when used in cooking. Always choose a luxury cooking white chocolate to avoid problems, and take great care not to overheat when melting. White chocolate is useful for color contrast, especially when decorating cakes.*

Couverture, *although this is the preferred chocolate for professionals (it retains a high gloss after melting and cooling), it requires tempering and is available only from specialty suppliers and has therefore not been used in this book.*

Chocolate-flavored Cake Covering *is an inferior product not generally used by true chocolate lovers. However, it has a higher fat content, making it easier to handle when making some decorations, such as curls or caraque. If you do not want to compromise the flavor too much, but have difficulty making the decorations with pure chocolate, try adding a few squares of chocolate-flavored cake covering to a good quality chocolate.*

Chocolate Chips *are available in dark, milk, and white chocolate varieties and are used for baking and decoration.*

Unsweetened Cocoa *is the powder left after the cocoa butter has been pressed from the roasted and ground beans. It is unsweetened and bitter in flavor. It gives a good, strong chocolate flavor when used in cooking.*

Cakes & Gateaux

It is hard to resist the pleasure of a sumptuous piece of chocolate cake and no chocolate book would be complete without a selection of family cakes and gateaux – there are plenty to choose from in this chapter. You can spend several indulgent hours in the kitchen making that perfect extravagant gateau or pop into the kitchen to knock up a quick cake for afternoon tea, the choice is yours. The more experimental among you can vary the fillings or decorations used according to what takes your fancy.

Alternatively, follow our easy step-by-step instructions and look at our glossy pictures to guide you to perfect results. The gateaux in this book will be perfectly at home on the dessert table – they are a feast for the eyes and will keep all hardened chocoholics in ecstasy. The family cakes are ideal for those who find a slice of chocolate cake comforting at any time, as many of them are made with surprising ease. So next time you feel like an indulgent slice of melt-in-the-mouth chocolate cake look no further.

Chocolate Almond Cake

Serves 8–10

INGREDIENTS

6 ounces dark chocolate	1¼ cups ground almonds	TO DECORATE:
¾ cup butter	1 tsp almond extract	2 tbsp toasted slivered almonds
⅔ cup superfine sugar		1 ounce dark chocolate, melted
4 eggs, separated	TOPPING:	
¼ tsp cream of tartar	4½ ounces milk chocolate	
⅓ cup self-rising flour	2 tbsp butter	
	4 tbsp heavy cream	

1 Lightly grease and flour the base of a 9-inch round springform pan. Break the chocolate into small pieces and place in a small pan with the butter. Heat gently, stirring until melted and well combined.

2 Place 7 tbsp of the superfine sugar in a bowl with the egg yolks and beat until the mixture is pale and creamy. Add the melted chocolate mixture, beating until well combined.

3 Sift the cream of tartar and flour together and fold into the chocolate mixture, together with the ground almonds and almond extract.

4 Beat the egg whites in a bowl until standing in soft peaks. Add the remaining superfine sugar and beat for about 2 minutes by hand, or 45–60 seconds if using an electric mixer, until thick and glossy. Carefully fold the egg whites into the chocolate mixture and spoon into the pan. Bake in a preheated oven at 375°F for 40 minutes, until just springy to the touch. Let cool.

5 Heat the topping ingredients in a double boiler. Remove from the heat and beat for 2 minutes. Chill in the refrigerator for 30 minutes. Transfer the cake to a plate and spread with the topping. Scatter with the almonds and drizzle with melted chocolate. Allow to set for 2 hours before serving.

Chocolate Tray Bake

Serves 15

INGREDIENTS

1 cup superfine sugar
1 cup soft margarine
4 eggs, beaten
4 tbsp milk
3 cups self-rising flour, sifted
3 tbsp cocoa powder, sifted

$\frac{1}{3}$ cup milk chocolate chips
$\frac{1}{3}$ cup dark chocolate chips
$\frac{1}{3}$ cup white chocolate chips
confectioners' sugar, to dust

1 Grease a $13 \times 9 \times 2$ inch cake pan with a little butter or margarine.

2 Place all the ingredients in the order listed, except the chocolate chips and confectioners' sugar, in a large mixing bowl and beat together until smooth.

3 Beat in the milk, dark, and white chocolate chips.

4 Spoon the mixture into the prepared cake pan and level the surface.

Bake in a preheated oven at 350°F for 30–40 minutes, until risen and springy to the touch. Cool in the pan.

5 Once cool, dust with confectioners' sugar. Cut into squares to serve.

COOK'S TIP

If desired, serve warm with cream for a delicious dessert.

COOK'S TIP

The cake can be frozen, wrapped in the pan, for 2 months. Thaw at room temperature.

VARIATION

For an attractive finish, cut thin strips of paper and lay in a criss-cross pattern on top of the cake. Dust with confectioners' sugar, then remove the paper strips.

Low-fat Chocolate & Pineapple Cake

Serves 9

INGREDIENTS

²/₃ cup low-fat spread
4¹/₂ ounces superfine sugar
³/₄ cup self-rising flour, sifted
3 tbsp unsweetened cocoa, sifted
1¹/₂ tsp baking powder
2 eggs

8 ounce can pineapple pieces in
    natural juice
¹/₂ cup low-fat thick unsweetened
    yogurt
about 1 tbsp confectioners' sugar
grated chocolate, to decorate

1 Lightly grease an 8-inch square cake pan.

2 Place the low-fat spread, superfine sugar, flour, unsweetened cocoa, baking powder, and eggs in a large mixing bowl. Beat with a wooden spoon or electric beater until smooth.

3 Pour the cake mixture into the prepared pan and level the surface. Bake in a preheated oven at 325°F for 20–25 minutes, or until springy to the touch.

Cool slightly in the pan before transferring to a wire rack to cool completely.

4 Drain the pineapple, chop the pineapple pieces, and drain again. Reserve a little of the pineapple for decoration, then stir the rest into the yogurt and sweeten to taste with confectioners' sugar.

5 Spread the pineapple and yogurt mixture over the cake and decorate with the reserved pineapple

pieces. Sprinkle with the grated chocolate.

COOK'S TIP

Store the cake, undecorated, in an airtight container for up to 3 days. Once decorated, refrigerate and use within 2 days.

Chocolate & Orange Cake

Serves 8–10

INGREDIENTS

³/₄ cup superfine sugar
³/₄ cup butter or margarine
3 eggs, beaten
1¹/₂ cups self-rising flour, sifted

2 tbsp unsweetened cocoa, sifted
2 tbsp milk
3 tbsp orange juice
grated rind of ¹/₂ orange

FROSTING:
1 cup confectioners' sugar
2 tbsp orange juice

1 Lightly grease a deep 8-inch round cake pan.

2 Beat together the sugar and butter or margarine in a bowl until light and fluffy. Gradually add the eggs, beating well after each addition. Carefully fold in the flour.

3 Divide the mixture in half. Add the unsweetened cocoa and milk to one half, stirring until combined. Flavor the other half with the orange juice and rind.

4 Spoon each mixture into the prepared pan and swirl together with a toothpick, to create a marbled effect. Bake in a preheated oven at 375°F for 25 minutes, or until springy to the touch.

5 Allow the cake to cool in the pan for a few minutes before transferring to a wire rack to cool completely.

6 To make the frosting, sift the confectioners' sugar into a mixing bowl and mix in enough of the orange juice to form a smooth frosting. Spread the frosting over the top of the cake and allow to set before serving.

VARIATION

Add 2 tablespoons of rum or brandy to the chocolate mixture instead of the milk. The cake also works well when flavored with grated lemon rind and juice.

Family Chocolate Cake

Serves 8–10

INGREDIENTS

1/2 cup soft margarine
2/3 cup superfine sugar
2 eggs
1 tbsp light corn syrup
1 cup self-rising flour, sifted
2 tbsp unsweetened cocoa, sifted

FILLING AND TOPPING:
1/4 cup confectioners' sugar, sifted
2 tbsp butter
3 1/2 ounces white or milk chocolate
a little milk or white chocolate,
    melted (optional)

1 Lightly grease two shallow 7-inch cake pans.

2 Place all the ingredients for the cake in a large mixing bowl and beat with a wooden spoon or electric mixer to form a smooth mixture.

3 Divide the mixture between the prepared pans and level the tops. Bake in a preheated oven at 325°F for 20 minutes, or until springy to the touch. Cool for a few minutes in the pans before transferring to a wire rack to cool completely.

4 To make the filling, beat the confectioners' sugar and butter together in a bowl until light and fluffy. Melt the chocolate and beat half into the frosting mixture. Use the filling to sandwich the cakes together.

5 Spread the remaining melted cooking chocolate over the top of the cake. Pipe circles of contrasting melted milk or white chocolate and feather into the chocolate with a toothpick, if preferred. Allow to set before serving.

COOK'S TIP

Eat this cake on the day of baking, as it does not keep well.

Chocolate & Vanilla Loaf Cake

Serves 10

INGREDIENTS

³/₄ cup superfine sugar
³/₄ cup soft margarine
¹/₂ tsp vanilla extract
3 eggs

2 cups self-rising flour, sifted
1³/₄ ounces dark chocolate
confectioners' sugar, to dust

1 Lightly grease a 1-pound loaf pan.

2 Beat together the sugar and soft margarine in a bowl until light and fluffy.

3 Beat in the vanilla extract. Gradually add the eggs, beating thoroughly after each addition. Carefully fold in the sifted flour.

4 Divide the mixture in half. Melt the dark chocolate and stir into one half of the mixture until well combined.

5 Place the vanilla mixture in the pan and level the top. Spread the chocolate layer over the vanilla layer.

6 Bake in a preheated oven at 375°F for 30 minutes, or until springy to the touch.

7 Cool the cake in the pan for a few minutes before transferring to a wire rack to cool completely.

8 Serve the cake lightly dusted with a little confectioners' sugar, if you wish.

COOK'S TIP

Freeze the cake undecorated for up to 2 months. Thaw at room temperature.

VARIATION

If desired, the mixtures can be marbled together with a toothpick.

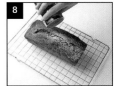

Chocolate Tea Bread

Serves 10

INGREDIENTS

³/₄ cup butter, softened	8 ounces dark chocolate chips	finely grated rind of 1 orange
¹/₂ cup light brown sugar	¹/₂ cup raisins	2 cups self-rising flour
4 eggs, lightly beaten	¹/₂ cup chopped walnuts	

1 Lightly grease a 2-pound loaf pan and line the base with baking parchment.

2 Cream together the butter and sugar in a bowl until light and fluffy.

3 Gradually add the eggs, beating well after each addition. If the mixture begins to curdle, beat in 1-2 tablespoons of the flour.

4 Stir in the chocolate chips, raisins, walnuts, and orange rind. Sift the flour and carefully fold it into the mixture.

5 Spoon the mixture into the prepared loaf pan and make a slight dip in the center of the top with the back of a spoon.

6 Bake in a preheated oven at 325°F for about 1 hour, or until a toothpick inserted into the center of the loaf comes out clean.

7 Cool in the pan for 5 minutes before carefully turning out and leaving on a wire rack to cool completely.

8 Serve the sweet bread cut into thin slices.

VARIATION

Use white or milk chocolate chips instead of dark chocolate chips, or a mixture of all three, if desired. Dried cranberries instead of the raisins also work well in this recipe.

COOK'S TIP

This sweet bread can be frozen, well wrapped, for up to 3 months. Thaw at room temperature.

Apricot & Chocolate Ring

Serves 12

INGREDIENTS

⅓ cup butter, diced
4 cups self-rising flour, sifted
4 tbsp superfine sugar
2 eggs, beaten
⅔ cup milk

FILLING AND DECORATION:
2 tbsp butter, melted
⅔ cup no-need-to-soak dried
    apricots, chopped
3½ ounces dark chocolate chips
1–2 tbsp milk, to glaze
1 ounce dark chocolate, melted

1 Grease a 10-inch round cake pan and line the base with baking parchment.

2 Rub the butter into the flour until the mixture resembles fine breadcrumbs. Stir in the superfine sugar, eggs, and milk to form a soft dough.

3 Roll out the dough on a lightly floured surface to form a 14-inch square.

4 Brush the melted butter over the surface of the dough. Mix together the apricots and chocolate chips and spread them over the dough to within 1 inch of the top and bottom.

5 Roll up the dough tightly, like a jelly roll, and cut it into 1-inch slices. Stand the slices in a ring around the edge of the prepared pan at a slight tilt. Brush with a little milk.

6 Bake in a preheated oven at 350°F for 30 minutes, or until cooked and golden. Cool the cake in the pan for about 15 minutes, then carefully transfer to a wire rack to cool.

7 Drizzle the melted chocolate over the ring, to decorate.

COOK'S TIP

This cake is best served very fresh, ideally on the day it is made. It is fabulous served slightly warm.

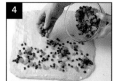

Chocolate Fruit Loaf

Serves 10

INGREDIENTS

3 cups strong white flour
$\frac{1}{4}$ cup unsweetened cocoa
5 tsp superfine sugar
1 envelope active dry yeast
$\frac{1}{4}$ tsp salt
1 cup tepid water
2 tbsp butter, melted

5 tbsp candied cherries,
    roughly chopped
$\frac{1}{2}$ cup dark chocolate chips
$\frac{1}{3}$ cup golden raisins
$\frac{3}{4}$ cup no-need-to soak dried
    apricots, roughly chopped

GLAZE:
1 tbsp superfine sugar
1 tbsp water

1 Lightly grease a 2-pound loaf pan. Sift the flour and cocoa into a large mixing bowl. Stir in the sugar, yeast, and salt.

2 Mix together the tepid water and butter. Make a well in the center of the dry ingredients and add the liquid. Mix well with a wooden spoon, then use your hands to bring the dough together. Turn out onto a lightly floured surface and knead for 5 minutes, until a smooth elastic dough forms.

Return to a clean bowl, cover with a damp cloth, and set aside to rise in a warm place for about 1 hour, or until doubled in size.

3 Turn the dough out onto a floured surface and knead for 5 minutes. Roll out to a rectangle about $\frac{1}{2}$ inch thick and the same width as the length of the pan. Scatter the cherries, chocolate chips, golden raisins, and chopped apricots over the dough. Carefully roll up the dough,

like a jelly roll, enclosing the filling. Transfer to the loaf pan, cover with a damp dish cloth, and set aside to rise for 20 minutes, or until the top of the dough is level with the top of the pan.

4 To make the glaze, mix together the sugar and water, then brush it over the top of the loaf. Bake in a preheated oven at 400°F for 30 minutes, or until well risen. Serve warm.

Mocha Layer Cake

Serves 8–10

INGREDIENTS

2 cups self-rising flour
$^{1}/_{4}$ tsp baking powder
4 tbsp unsweetened cocoa
7 tbsp superfine sugar
2 eggs
2 tbsp light corn syrup
$^{2}/_{3}$ cup sunflower oil
$^{2}/_{3}$ cup milk

FILLING:
1 tsp instant coffee
1 tbsp boiling water
$1^{1}/_{4}$ cups heavy cream
2 tbsp confectioners' sugar

TO DECORATE:
$1^{3}/_{4}$ ounces dark chocolate to make curls (see page 66)
chocolate caraque (see page 208)
confectioners' sugar, to dust

1 Lightly grease three 7-inch cake pans.

2 Sift the flour, baking powder, and unsweetened cocoa into a large mixing bowl. Stir in the sugar. Make a well in the center and stir in the eggs, syrup, oil, and milk. Beat with a wooden spoon, gradually mixing in the dry ingredients to make a smooth batter. Divide the mixture between the prepared pans.

3 Bake in a preheated oven at 350°F for 35–45 minutes, or until springy to the touch. Leave the cakes in the pans for 5 minutes, then turn out onto a wire rack to cool completely.

4 Dissolve the instant coffee in the boiling water and place in a bowl with the cream and confectioners' sugar. Whip until the cream is just holding its shape. Use half the cream to sandwich the 3 cakes together. Spread the

remaining cream over the top and sides of the cake. Lightly press the chocolate curls into the cream around the edge of the cake.

5 Transfer to a serving plate. Lay the caraque over the top of the cake. Cut a few thin strips of baking parchment and place on top of the caraque. Dust lightly with confectioners' sugar, then carefully remove the paper. Serve.

Chocolate Lamington Pound Cake

Serves 8–10

INGREDIENTS

³/₄ cup butter or margarine
³/₄ cup superfine sugar
3 eggs, lightly beaten
1¹/₄ cups self-rising flour

2 tbsp unsweetened cocoa
1³/₄ ounces dark chocolate, broken
    into pieces
5 tbsp milk

1 tsp butter
³/₄ cup confectioners' sugar
about 8 tbsp shredded coconut
²/₃ cup heavy cream, whipped

1 Lightly grease a 1-pound loaf pan – preferably a long, thin pan about 3 × 10 inches.

2 Cream together the butter and sugar in a bowl until light and fluffy. Gradually add the eggs, beating well after each addition. Sift together the flour and cocoa. Fold into the mixture.

3 Pour the mixture into the prepared pan and level the top. Bake in a preheated oven at 350°F for 40 minutes, or until springy to the touch. Cool the cake for 5 minutes in the pan, then turn out onto a wire rack to cool completely.

4 Place the chocolate, milk, and butter in a double boiler. Stir until the chocolate has melted. Add the confectioners' sugar and beat until smooth. Cool until the frosting is thick enough to spread, then spread it all over the cake. Sprinkle with the shredded coconut and allow the frosting to set.

5 Cut a V-shape wedge from the top of the cake and set aside. Put the cream in a pastry bag fitted with a plain or star tip. Pipe the cream down the center of the V-shaped gap and replace the wedge of cake on top of the cream. Pipe another line of cream along either side of the wedge of cake. Serve.

Rich Chocolate Layer Cake

Serves 10–12

INGREDIENTS

7 eggs
1¾ cups superfine sugar
1¼ cups all-purpose flour
½ cup unsweetened cocoa
4 tbsp butter, melted

FILLING:
7 ounces dark chocolate
½ cup butter
4 tbsp confectioners' sugar

TO DECORATE:
⅔ cup toasted slivered almonds,
   lightly crushed
small chocolate curls (see page 214)
   or grated chocolate

1 Grease a deep 9-inch square cake pan and line the base with baking parchment.

2 Beat the eggs and superfine sugar in a mixing bowl with an electric beater for about 10 minutes, or until the mixture is very light and foamy and the beater leaves a trail that lasts a few seconds when lifted.

3 Sift the flour and cocoa together and fold half into the mixture. Drizzle the melted butter over it and fold in the rest of the flour and cocoa. Pour into the prepared pan and bake in a preheated oven at 350°F for 30–35 minutes, or until springy to the touch. Cool slightly, then remove from the pan and cool completely on a wire rack.

4 To make the filling, melt the chocolate and butter together, then remove from the heat. Stir in the confectioners' sugar, let cool, then beat until thick enough to spread.

5 Halve the cake lengthwise and cut each half into 3 layers. Sandwich the layers together with three-quarters of the chocolate filling. Spread the remainder over the cake and mark a wavy pattern on the top. Press the almonds onto the sides. Decorate with chocolate curls or grated chocolate.

Chocolate & Mango Layer Cake

Serves 12

INGREDIENTS

½ cup unsweetened cocoa	2½ cups self-rising flour	2¾ ounces dark chocolate, curled,
⅔ cup boiling water	2 x 14 ounce cans mango	or grated chocolate
6 large eggs	1 tsp cornstarch	
1½ cups superfine sugar	1¾ cups heavy cream	

1 Grease a deep 9-inch round cake pan and line the base with baking parchment.

2 Place the unsweetened cocoa in a small bowl and gradually add the boiling water; blend to form a smooth paste.

3 Place the eggs and superfine sugar in a mixing bowl and beat until the mixture is very light and foamy and the beater leaves a trail that lasts a few seconds when lifted. Fold in the cocoa mixture. Sift the flour and carefully fold it into the mixture.

4 Pour the mixture into the pan and level the top. Bake in a preheated oven at 325°F for about 1 hour or until springy to the touch.

5 Cool in the pan for a few minutes, then turn out and cool completely on a wire rack. Peel off the lining paper and cut the cake into 3 layers.

6 Drain the mangoes and place a quarter of them in a food processor and process until smooth. Mix the cornstarch with about 3 tbsp of the mango juice to form a smooth paste. Add to the mango purée. Transfer to a small pan and heat gently, stirring until the purée thickens. Let cool.

7 Chop the remaining mango. Whip the cream and reserve about one quarter. Fold the mango into the remaining cream and use to sandwich the layers of cake together. Place on a serving plate. Spread some of the remaining cream around the side of the cake. Press the curled or grated chocolate lightly into the cream. Pipe cream rosettes around the top. Spread the mango purée over the center.

Devil's Food Cake

Serves 8

INGREDIENTS

3½ ounces dark chocolate
2¼ cups self-rising flour
1 tsp baking soda
1 cup butter

2⅔ cups dark brown sugar
1 tsp vanilla extract
3 eggs
½ cup buttermilk
2 cups boiling water

FROSTING:
1½ cups superfine sugar
2 egg whites
1 tbsp lemon juice
3 tbsp orange juice
candied orange peel, to decorate

1 Lightly grease and flour two shallow 8-inch round cake pans. Melt the chocolate in a pan. Sift the flour and baking soda together.

2 Beat the butter and dark brown sugar in a bowl until pale and fluffy. Beat in the vanilla extract and the eggs, one at a time and beating well after each addition. Add a little extra flour if the mixture is beginning to curdle.

3 Fold the melted chocolate into the mixture until well blended. Gradually fold in the remaining flour, then stir in the buttermilk and boiling water.

4 Divide the mixture between the pans and level the tops. Bake in a preheated oven at 375°F for 30 minutes, until springy to the touch. Cool the cakes in the pans for 5 minutes, then transfer to a wire rack to cool completely.

5 Place the frosting ingredients in a double boiler over gently simmering water. Beat, preferably with an electric beater, until thickened and forming soft peaks. Remove from the heat and beat until the mixture is cool.

6 Sandwich the 2 cakes together with a little of the frosting, then spread the remainder over the sides and top of the cake, swirling it as you do so. Decorate with the candied orange peel.

Chocolate Carrot Cake

Serves 10–12

INGREDIENTS

5 eggs	6 ounces carrots, peeled and finely	12 ounces cream cheese
²/₃ cup superfine sugar	grated	1 cup confectioners' sugar
1¼ cups all-purpose flour	½ cup chopped walnuts	6 ounces milk or dark
⅓ cup unsweetened cocoa	2 tbsp sunflower oil	chocolate, melted

1 Lightly grease and flour the base of a deep 8-inch round cake pan.

2 Place the eggs and sugar in a double boiler over gently simmering water and beat until very thick. Lift the whisk up and let the mixture drizzle back – it will leave a trail for a few seconds when thick enough.

3 Remove from the heat. Sift the flour and unsweetened cocoa into the mixture and carefully fold in. Gently fold in the carrots, walnuts, and oil until just combined.

4 Pour into the prepared pan and bake in a preheated oven at 375°F for 45 minutes, or until well risen and springy to the touch. Cool the cake slightly, then turn out onto a wire rack to cool completely.

5 Beat together the cheese and confectioners' sugar until combined. Beat in the melted chocolate. Split the cake in half and sandwich together again with half the chocolate mixture. Cover the top of the cake with the remainder of the chocolate mixture, swirling it with a knife. Chill or serve at once.

COOK'S TIP

The undecorated cake can be frozen for up to 2 months. Thaw at room temperature for 3 hours or overnight in the refrigerator.

Chocolate Yogurt Cake

Serves 8-10

INGREDIENTS

²/₃ cup vegetable oil
²/₃ cup whole milk
    unsweetened yogurt
1¼ cups light brown sugar
3 eggs, beaten
¾ cup whole-wheat self-rising
    flour

1 cup self-rising flour, sifted
2 tbsp unsweetened cocoa
1 tsp baking soda
1¾ ounces dark chocolate, melted

FILLING:
²/₃ cup whole milk
    unsweetened yogurt
²/₃ cup heavy cream
8 ounces fresh soft fruit, such as
    strawberries or raspberries

1 Grease a deep 9-inch round cake pan and line the base with baking parchment.

2 Place the oil, yogurt, sugar, and beaten eggs in a large mixing bowl and beat together until well combined. Sift the flours, unsweetened cocoa, and baking soda together and beat into the bowl until thoroughly combined. Beat in the melted dark chocolate.

3 Pour the mixture into the prepared pan and bake in a preheated oven at 350°F for 45–50 minutes, or until a toothpick inserted into the center comes out clean. Cool in the pan for 5 minutes, then turn out onto a wire rack to cool completely. When cold, divide the cake into 3 layers.

4 Place the yogurt and cream in a large mixing bowl and beat well until the mixture stands in soft peaks.

5 Place one layer of cake onto a serving plate and spread with some of the cream. Top with a little of the fruit (slicing larger fruit such as strawberries). Repeat with the next layer. Top with the final layer of cake and spread with the rest of the cream. Arrange more fruit on top and cut the cake into wedges to serve.

Chocolate Layer Log

Serves 8–10

INGREDIENTS

1/2 cup soft margarine
1/2 cup superfine sugar
2 eggs
3/4 cup self-rising flour
1/4 cup unsweetened cocoa
2 tbsp milk

WHITE CHOCOLATE BUTTER CREAM:
2 3/4 ounces white chocolate
2 tbsp milk
2/3 cup butter 3/4 cup confectioners' sugar
2 tbsp orange-flavored liqueur

large dark chocolate curls
(see page 66), to decorate

1 Grease and flour the sides of two clean, dry 14-ounce food cans.

2 Beat together the margarine and sugar in a bowl until light and fluffy. Gradually add the eggs, beating well after each addition. Sift together the flour and unsweetened cocoa and fold into the cake mixture. Fold in the milk.

3 Divide the mixture between the two prepared cans. Stand the cans on a cookie sheet and bake in a preheated oven at

350°F for 40 minutes, or until springy to the touch. Cool the cakes for about 5 minutes in the cans, then turn out and cool completely on a wire rack.

4 To make the butter cream, put the chocolate and milk in a pan and heat gently until the chocolate has melted, stirring until well combined. Let cool slightly. Beat together the butter and confectioners' sugar until light and fluffy. Beat in the orange liqueur. Gradually beat in the chocolate mixture.

5 To assemble, cut both cakes into 1/2-inch-thick slices, then reassemble them by sandwiching the slices together with some of the butter cream.

6 Place the cake on a serving plate and spread the remaining butter cream over the top and sides. Decorate with the chocolate curls, then serve the cake cut diagonally into slices.

Chocolate & Orange Mousse Cake

Serves 12

INGREDIENTS

¾ cup butter
¾ cup superfine sugar
4 eggs, lightly beaten
1¾ cups self-raising flour
1 tbsp cocoa powder
1¾ oz dark orange-flavoured
   chocolate, melted

ORANGE MOUSSE:
2 eggs, separated
4 tbsp superfine sugar
¾ cup freshly squeezed orange
   juice
2 tsp gelatine
3 tbsp water

¼ cups heavy cream
peeled orange slices, to decorate

1 Grease a 20 cm/8 inch springform cake pan and and line the base. Beat the butter and sugar in a bowl until light and fluffy. Gradually add the eggs, beating well after each addition. strain together the cocoa and flour and fold into the cake mixture. Fold in the chocolate.

2 Pour into the prepared pan and level the top. Bake in a preheated oven, 180°C/350°F/Gas Mark 4, for 40 minutes or until springy to the touch. Leave to cool for 5 minutes in the pan,

then turn out and leave to cool completely on a wire rack. Cut the cold cake into 2 layers.

3 To make the orange mousse, beat the egg yolks and sugar until light, then whisk in the orange juice. Sprinkle the gelatine over the water in a small bowl and allow to go spongy, then place over a pan of hot water and stir until dissolved. Stir into the mousse.

4 Whip the cream until holding its shape, reserve a little for decoration

and fold the rest into the mousse. Whisk the egg whites until standing in soft peaks, then fold in. Leave in a cool place until starting to set, stirring occasionally.

5 Place half of the cake in the pan. Pour in the mousse and press the second cake layer on top. Chill until set. Transfer to a dish, pipe cream rosettes on the top and arrange orange slices in the centre.

Chocolate Roulade

Serves 6–8

INGREDIENTS

5¹/₂ ounces dark chocolate
2 tbsp water
6 eggs
³/₄ cup superfine sugar
¹/₄ cup all-purpose flour
1 tbsp unsweetened cocoa

FILLING:
1¹/₄ cups heavy cream
2³/₄ ounces sliced strawberries

TO DECORATE:
confectioners' sugar
chocolate leaves (see below)

1 Line a 15 × 10 inch jelly roll pan with baking parchment. Melt the chocolate in the water, stirring. Let cool slightly.

2 Place the eggs and sugar in a bowl and beat for 10 minutes, or until the mixture is pale and foamy and the beater leaves a trail when lifted. Beat in the melted chocolate in a thin stream. Sift the flour and cocoa together and fold into the mixture. Pour into the pan and level the top.

3 Bake in a preheated oven at 400°F for 12 minutes. Dust a sheet of baking parchment with a little confectioners' sugar. Turn out the roulade and remove the lining paper. Roll up the roulade with the fresh parchment inside. Place on a wire rack, cover with a damp dish cloth, and let cool.

4 Beat the cream until just holding its shape. Unroll the roulade, remove the paper, and scatter the fruit over it. Spread three quarters of the cream over the roulade and re-roll. Dust with confectioners' sugar. Place the roulade on a plate. Pipe the rest of the cream down the center and decorate with chocolate leaves.

5 To make chocolate leaves, wash some rose or holly leaves and pat dry with paper towels. Melt some chocolate and brush it over the leaves. Set aside to harden. Repeat with 2–3 layers of chocolate. Peel the leaves away from the chocolate.

Chocolate & Coconut Roulade

Serves 8–10

INGREDIENTS

3 eggs
¹/₃ cup superfine sugar
¹/₃ cup self-rising flour
1 tbsp block creamed coconut,
    softened with 1 tbsp boiling water
1 cup shredded coconut
6 tbsp good raspberry conserve

CHOCOLATE COATING:
7 ounces dark chocolate
¹/₄ cup butter
2 tbsp light corn syrup

RASPBERRY COULIS:
1¹/₃ cups fresh or frozen raspberries,
    thawed if frozen
2 tbsp water
4 tbsp confectioners' sugar

1 Grease and line a 9 × 12 inch jelly roll pan. Beat together the eggs and superfine sugar in a large mixing bowl with an electric mixer for about 10 minutes, or until the mixture is very light and foamy and the beater leaves a trail that will last a few seconds when lifted.

2 Sift the flour and fold in with a metal spoon or a spatula. Fold in the creamed coconut and shredded coconut. Pour into the prepared pan and bake in a preheated oven at 400°F for about 10–12 minutes, or until springy to the touch.

3 Sprinkle a sheet of baking parchment with a little superfine sugar and place on top of a damp dish cloth. Turn the cake out onto the paper and carefully peel away the lining paper. Spread the conserve over the sponge cake and roll up from the short end, using the dish cloth to help you. Place seam side down on a wire rack and cool completely.

4 To make the coating, melt the chocolate and butter, stirring constantly. Stir in the light corn syrup and set aside to cool for 5 minutes. Spread it over the roulade and allow to set. To make the coulis, purée the fruit in a food processor with the water and sugar; run through a strainer to remove the seeds. Cut the roulade into slices and serve with the coulis.

Almond & Hazelnut Cake

Serves 8–10

INGREDIENTS

4 eggs
7 tbsp superfine sugar
$\frac{1}{2}$ cup ground almonds
$\frac{1}{2}$ cup ground hazelnuts
$\frac{1}{3}$ cup all-purpose flour
$\frac{1}{2}$ cup slivered almonds

FILLING:
$3\frac{1}{2}$ ounces dark chocolate
1 tbsp butter
$1\frac{1}{4}$ cups heavy cream
confectioners' sugar, to dust

1 Grease two 7-inch round sponge cake layer pans and line the bases with sheets of baking parchment.

2 Beat the eggs and superfine sugar together in a large mixing bowl with an electric mixer for about 10 minutes, or until the mixture is very light and foamy and the beater leaves a trail that lasts a few seconds when lifted.

3 Fold in the ground nuts, sift the flour and fold in with a metal spoon or spatula. Pour into the prepared pans.

4 Scatter the slivered almonds over the top of one of the cakes. Bake both cakes in a preheated oven at 375°F for 15–20 minutes, or until springy to the touch.

5 Cool the cakes slightly in the pans. Carefully remove the cakes from the pans and transfer them to a wire rack to cool completely.

6 To make the filling, melt the chocolate, remove from the heat, and stir in the butter. Let cool slightly. Whip the cream until just holding its shape, then fold in the melted chocolate until mixed.

7 Place the cake without the extra almonds on a serving plate and spread the filling over it. Allow to set slightly, then place the almond-topped cake on top of the filling and chill for about 1 hour. Dust with confectioners' sugar and serve.

Chocolate & Walnut Cake

Serves 8–12

INGREDIENTS

4 eggs
1/2 cup superfine sugar
1 cup all-purpose flour
1 tbsp unsweetened cocoa

2 tbsp butter, melted
2 3/4 ounces dark chocolate, melted
1 1/4 cups finely chopped walnuts

FROSTING:
2 3/4 ounces dark chocolate
1/2 cup butter
1 1/4 cups confectioners' sugar
2 tbsp milk
walnut halves, to decorate

1 Grease a deep 7-inch round cake pan and line the base. Place the eggs and superfine sugar in a mixing bowl and beat with an electric mixer for 10 minutes, or until the mixture is light and foamy and the beater leaves a trail that lasts a few seconds when lifted.

2 Sift together the flour and unsweetened cocoa and fold in with a metal spoon or spatula. Fold in the melted butter and chocolate, and the chopped walnuts. Pour into the prepared pan and bake in a preheated oven at 325°F for 30–35 minutes, or until springy to the touch.

3 Cool the cake in the pan for 5 minutes, then transfer to a wire rack to cool completely. Cut the cold cake into 2 layers.

4 To make the frosting, melt the dark chocolate and let cool slightly. Beat together the butter, confectioners' sugar, and milk in a bowl until the mixture is pale and fluffy. Beat in the melted chocolate.

5 Sandwich the 2 cake layers with some of the frosting and then transfer to a serving plate. Spread the remaining frosting over the top of the cake with a spatula, swirling it slightly as you do so to make a pattern. Decorate the cake with the walnut halves and serve.

Dobos Torte

Serves 8

INGREDIENTS

3 eggs	FILLING:	CARAMEL:
7 tbsp superfine sugar	6 ounces dark chocolate	7 tbsp sugar
1 tsp vanilla extract	³/₄ cup butter	4 tbsp water
¹/₂ cup all-purpose flour	2 tbsp milk	
	2 cups confectioners' sugar	

1 Draw four 7-inch circles on sheets of baking parchment. Place 2 of them upside down on 2 cookie sheets. Beat the eggs and superfine sugar in a large mixing bowl with an electric mixer for 10 minutes, or until the mixture is light and foamy and the beater leaves a trail that lasts for a few seconds when lifted. Fold in the vanilla extract. Sift the flour and fold in with a metal spoon or a spatula. Spoon a quarter of the mixture onto one of the sheets and spread out to the size of the circle. Repeat with the other circle. Bake in a preheated oven at 400°F for 5–8 minutes, or until golden brown. Cool on wire racks. Repeat with the remaining mixture.

2 To make the filling, melt the chocolate and cool slightly. Beat the butter, milk, and confectioners' sugar until pale and fluffy. Beat in the chocolate. Place the sugar and water for the caramel in a heavy-based pan and heat gently, stirring until the sugar dissolves. Boil gently until the syrup is pale golden. Remove the pan from the heat. Pour the caramel over one layer of the cake to cover the top. Allow to harden slightly, then mark into 8 portions with an oiled knife. Remove the cakes from the paper and trim the edges. Sandwich the layers together with some of the filling, finishing with the caramel-topped cake. Place on a serving plate and spread the sides with the filling mixture. Pipe rosettes around the top of the cake. Cut into slices to serve.

Bistvitny Torte

Serves 10

INGREDIENTS

CHOCOLATE TRIANGLES:
1 ounce dark chocolate, melted
1 ounce white chocolate, melted

CAKE:
3/4 cup soft margarine
3/4 cup superfine sugar
1/2 tsp vanilla extract
3 eggs, lightly beaten
2 cups self-rising flour
1 3/4 ounces dark chocolate

SYRUP:
1/2 cup sugar
6 tbsp water
3 tbsp brandy or sherry
2/3 cup heavy cream

1 Grease a 9-inch ring pan. To make the triangles, place a sheet of baking parchment onto a cookie sheet and place alternate spoonfuls of the dark and white chocolate onto the paper. Spread together to form a thick marbled layer. Allow to set. Cut into squares, then into triangles.

2 To make the cake, beat the margarine and sugar until light and fluffy. Beat in the vanilla extract. Gradually add the eggs, beating well after each addition. Carefully fold in the flour.

Divide the mixture in half. Melt the dark chocolate and stir into one half.

3 Spoon each mixture into the prepared pan and swirl together with a toothpick to create a marbled effect.

4 Bake in a preheated oven at 375°F for 30 minutes, or until the cake is springy to the touch. Cool in the pan for a few minutes, then transfer to a wire rack to cool completely.

5 To make the syrup, place the sugar in a small pan with the water and heat, stirring until the sugar has dissolved. Boil for 1–2 minutes. Remove the pan from the heat and stir in the brandy or sherry. Let the syrup cool slightly then gradually spoon it over the cake, allowing it to soak into the sponge cake. Whip the cream and pipe swirls of it on top of the cake. Finally, decorate with the chocolate triangles.

Sachertorte

Serves 10–12

INGREDIENTS

6 ounces dark chocolate
²/₃ cup sweet butter
²/₃ cup superfine sugar
6 eggs, separated
1¼ cups all-purpose flour

FROSTING AND FILLING:
6 ounces dark chocolate
5 tbsp strong black coffee

1 cup confectioners' sugar
6 tbsp apricot preserve
1¾ ounces dark chocolate, melted

1 Grease a 9-inch springform cake pan and flour the base. Melt the chocolate. Beat together the butter and ⅔ cup of the sugar until pale and fluffy. Add the egg yolks and beat thoroughly. Add the chocolate in a thin continuous stream, beating well. Sift the flour and fold it into the mixture. Beat the egg whites until they stand in soft peaks. Add the remaining sugar and whisk for 2 minutes by hand, or 45-60 seconds if using an electric mixer, until glossy. Fold half into the chocolate mixture, then fold in the remainder.

2 Spoon into the prepared pan and level the top. Bake in a preheated oven at 300°F for 1–1¼ hours, until a toothpick inserted into the center comes out clean. Cool the cake in the pan for 5 minutes, then transfer to a wire rack to cool completely.

3 To make the frosting, melt the chocolate and beat in the coffee until smooth. Sift the confectioners' sugar into a bowl. Beat in the chocolate mixture to make a thick frosting. Halve the cake. Warm the preserve, spread over one half of the cake, and sandwich together.

Invert the cake on a wire rack. Spoon the frosting over the cake and spread to coat the top and sides. Allow to set for 5 minutes, allowing any excess frosting to drop through the rack. Transfer to a serving plate and allow to set for at least 2 hours.

4 To decorate, spoon the melted chocolate into a small pastry bag and pipe the word "Sacher" or "Sachertorte" on the top of the cake. Allow it to harden before serving the cake.

Dark & White Chocolate Torte

Serves 10

INGREDIENTS

4 eggs
½ cup superfine sugar
¾ cup all-purpose flour

DARK CHOCOLATE CREAM:
⅔ cup heavy cream
5½ ounces dark chocolate, broken into small pieces

WHITE CHOCOLATE FROSTING:
2¾ ounces white chocolate
1 tbsp butter
1 tbsp milk
4 tbsp confectioners' sugar
chocolate caraque (see page 208)

1 Grease an 8-inch round springform pan and line the base. Beat the eggs and superfine sugar in a large mixing bowl with an electric mixer for about 10 minutes, or until the mixture is very light and foamy and the beater leaves a trail that lasts a few seconds when lifted.

2 Sift the flour and fold in with a metal spoon or spatula. Pour into the prepared pan and bake in a preheated oven at 350°F for 35–40 minutes, or until springy to the touch. Cool

the cake slightly in the pan, then transfer to a wire rack to cool completely. Cut the cold cake into 2 layers.

3 To make the chocolate cream, place the cream in a saucepan and bring to a boil, stirring. Add the chocolate and stir until melted and well combined. Remove from the heat and let cool. Beat with a wooden spoon until the mixture starts to thicken.

4 Sandwich the 2 cake layers together with the chocolate cream and place on a wire rack.

5 To make the frosting, melt the chocolate and butter together and stir until thoroughly blended. Beat in the milk and confectioners' sugar. Beat for a few minutes, until the frosting is cool. Pour it over the cake and spread with a spatula to coat the top and sides. Decorate with chocolate caraque and allow to set.

Chocolate Ganache Cake

Serves 10–12

INGREDIENTS

³/₄ cup butter
³/₄ cup superfine sugar
4 eggs, lightly beaten
1³/₄ cups self-rising flour
1 tbsp unsweetened cocoa
1³/₄ ounces dark chocolate, melted

GANACHE:
2 cups heavy cream
13 ounces dark chocolate, broken
   into pieces

TO FINISH:
7 ounces chocolate-flavored cake
   covering or dark chocolate

1 Lightly grease an 8-inch springform cake pan and flour the base. Beat the butter and sugar until light and fluffy. Gradually add the eggs, beating well after each addition. Sift together the flour and cocoa. Carefully fold into the cake mixture. Fold in the melted chocolate.

2 Pour into the prepared pan and level the top. Bake in a preheated oven at 350°F for 40 minutes, or until springy to the touch. Allow the cake to cool for 5 minutes in the pan, then turn out onto a wire rack to cool completely. Cut the cold cake into 2 layers.

3 To make the ganache, place the cream in a pan and bring to a boil, stirring. Add the chocolate and stir until melted and combined. Pour into a bowl and beat for about 5 minutes, or until the ganache is fluffy and cool.

4 Reserve one-third of the ganache. Use the remaining ganache to sandwich the cake layers together and to spread over the top and sides of the cake.

5 Melt the cake covering or chocolate and spread it over a large sheet of baking parchment. Cool until just set. Cut into strips a little wider than the height of the cake and place around the edge of the cake, overlapping them slightly.

6 Pipe the reserved ganache in tear drops or shells over the top of the cake. Chill for 1 hour.

Yule Log

Serves 8–10

INGREDIENTS

CAKE:
4 eggs
½ cup superfine sugar
⅔ cup self-rising flour
2 tbsp unsweetened cocoa

FROSTING:
5½ ounces dark chocolate
2 egg yolks
⅔ cup milk
½ cup butter
4 tbsp confectioners' sugar
2 tbsp rum (optional)

TO DECORATE:
a little white glacé or royal frosting
confectioners' sugar, to dust
holly or Christmas cake decorations

1 Grease and line a 12 × 9 inch jelly roll pan. Beat the eggs and superfine sugar in a bowl with an electric mixer for 10 minutes, or until the mixture is very light and foamy and the beater leaves a trail. Sift the flour and unsweetened cocoa and fold in. Pour into the prepared pan and bake in a preheated oven at 400°F for 12 minutes, or until springy to the touch. Turn out onto a piece of baking parchment sprinkled with a little superfine sugar. Peel off the lining paper and trim the edges. Cut a small slit halfway into the cake about ½ inch from one short end. Starting at that end, roll up tightly, enclosing the paper. Place on a wire rack to cool.

2 To make the frosting, break the chocolate into pieces and melt in a double boiler. Beat in the egg yolks, then beat in the milk, and cook, stirring, until the mixture thickens enough to coat the back of a wooden spoon. Cover with dampened wax paper and cool. Beat the butter and sugar until pale and fluffy. Beat in the cooled mixture and rum, if using. Unroll the sponge cake, remove the paper, spread with one third of the frosting, and roll up again. Place on a serving plate. Spread the remaining frosting over the cake and mark with a fork to give the effect of bark. Allow to set. Pipe white frosting to form the rings of the log. Sprinkle with sugar and decorate.

Chocolate Truffle Cake

Serves 12

INGREDIENTS

¹/3 cup butter
¹/3 cup superfine sugar
2 eggs, lightly beaten
²/3 cup self-rising flour
¹/2 tsp baking powder
¹/4 cup unsweetened cocoa
¹/2 cup ground almonds

TRUFFLE TOPPING:
12 ounces dark chocolate
¹/2 cup butter
1¹/4 cups heavy cream
1¹/4 cups plain cake crumbs
3 tbsp dark rum

TO DECORATE:
ground cherries
1³/4 ounces dark chocolate, melted

1 Lightly grease an 8-inch round spring-form pan and flour the base. Beat together the butter and sugar until light and fluffy. Gradually add the eggs, beating well after each addition.

2 Sift the flour, baking powder, and unsweetened cocoa together and fold into the mixture, along with the ground almonds. Pour into the prepared pan and bake in a preheated oven at 350°F for 20–25 minutes, or until springy to the touch. Cool the cake slightly in the pan, then transfer to a wire rack to cool completely. Wash and dry the pan and return the cooled cake to it.

3 To make the topping, heat the chocolate, butter, and heavy cream in a heavy-based pan over a low heat and stir until smooth. Cool, then chill for 30 minutes. Beat well with a wooden spoon and chill for a further 30 minutes. Beat the mixture again, then add the cake crumbs and rum, beating until well combined. Spoon the topping over the sponge cake base and chill for 3 hours.

4 Meanwhile, dip the ground cherries in the melted chocolate until partially covered. Set on baking parchment. Transfer the cake to a serving plate; decorate with ground cherries.

White Chocolate Truffle Cake

Serves 12

INGREDIENTS

2 eggs
4 tbsp superfine sugar
1/3 cup all-purpose flour
1 3/4 ounces white chocolate, melted

TRUFFLE TOPPING:
1 1/4 cups heavy cream
12 ounces white chocolate, broken
    into pieces
1 1/4 cups cream cheese

TO DECORATE:
dark, milk, or white chocolate,
    melted
unsweetened cocoa, to dust

1 Grease an 8-inch round springform pan and flour the base. Beat the eggs and superfine sugar in a mixing bowl for 10 minutes, or until the mixture is very light and foamy and the whisk leaves a trail that lasts a few seconds when lifted. Sift the flour and carefully fold in with a metal spoon. Fold in the melted white chocolate. Pour the mixture into the prepared pan and bake in a preheated oven at 350°F for 25 minutes, or until springy to the touch. Cool slightly, then transfer to a wire rack to cool completely. Return the cold cake to the pan.

2 To make the truffle topping, place the cream in a pan and bring to a boil, stirring to prevent it from sticking to the bottom of the pan. Allow to cool slightly, then add the white chocolate pieces, and stir until melted and combined. Remove the pan from the heat and stir until almost cool, then stir in the cream cheese. Pour the mixture on top of the cake and chill for about 2 hours. Remove the cake from the pan and transfer to a serving plate.

3 To make large chocolate curls, pour melted chocolate onto a marble or acrylic board and spread it thinly with a spatula. Allow to set at room temperature. Using a peeler, push through the chocolate at a 25 degree angle until a large curl forms. Remove each curl as you make it and refrigerate until set. Decorate the cake with chocolate curls and sprinkle with a little unsweetened cocoa.

Chocolate & Raspberry Vacherin

Serves 10–12

INGREDIENTS

3 egg whites
¾ cup superfine sugar
1 tsp cornstarch
1 ounce dark chocolate, grated

FILLING:
6 ounces dark chocolate
2 cups heavy cream, whipped

2 cups fresh raspberries
a little melted chocolate, to
   decorate

1 Draw three rectangles, 4 × 10 inches, on sheets of baking parchment and place on 2 cookie sheets.

2 Beat the egg whites in a mixing bowl until standing in soft peaks, then gradually beat in half the sugar, and continue beating until the mixture is very stiff and glossy.

3 Carefully fold in the rest of the sugar, the cornstarch, and grated chocolate with a metal spoon or a spatula.

4 Spoon the meringue mixture into a pastry bag fitted with a ½-inch plain tip, and pipe lines across the rectangles.

5 Bake in a preheated oven at 275°F for 1½ hours, changing the positions of the cookie sheets halfway through. Without opening the oven door, turn off the oven and leave the meringues until they are completely cold, then peel away the paper.

6 To make the filling, melt the chocolate and spread it over 2 of the meringue layers. Leave the filling to harden.

7 Place 1 chocolate-coated meringue on a plate and top with about one-third of the cream and raspberries. Gently place the second chocolate-coated meringue on top and spread with half the remaining cream and raspberries.

8 Place the last meringue on the top and decorate it with the remaining cream and raspberries. Drizzle a little melted chocolate over the top and serve.

Tropical Fruit Vacherin

Serves 10–12

INGREDIENTS

6 egg whites
1¼ cups superfine sugar
¾ cup shredded coconut

FILLING AND TOPPING:
3 ounces dark chocolate, broken
into pieces
3 egg yolks
3 tbsp water

1 tbsp rum (optional)
4 tbsp superfine sugar
2 cups heavy cream
selection of tropical fruit, sliced or
cut into bite-size pieces

1 Draw three circles, 8 inches each, on sheets of baking parchment and place them on cookie sheets.

2 Beat the egg whites until standing in soft peaks, then gradually beat in half the sugar and continue beating until the mixture is very stiff and glossy. Carefully fold in the remaining sugar and the coconut.

3 Spoon the mixture into a pastry bag fitted with a star tip and cover the circles with piped swirls. Bake in a preheated oven at 275°F for 1½ hours, changing the position of the cookie sheets halfway through. Without opening the oven door, turn off the oven and leave the meringues until they have cooled completely, then peel away the paper.

4 To make the filling, place the chocolate pieces, egg yolks, water, rum, if using, and sugar in a double boiler over gently simmering water. Cook over a low heat, stirring, until the chocolate has melted and the mixture has thickened. Cover with a disc of baking parchment and set aside until cold.

5 Whip the cream and fold two thirds of it into the chocolate mixture. Sandwich the meringue layers together with the chocolate mixture. Place the remaining cream in a pastry bag fitted with a star tip and pipe around the edge of the meringue. Arrange the tropical fruits in the center.

Small Cakes & Cookies

This chapter contains everyday delights for chocolate
fans. You are sure to be tempted by our wonderful
array of cookies and small cakes. Make any day
special with a home-made chocolate cookie to be
served with coffee, as a snack or to accompany a
special dessert. Although some take a little longer to
make, most are quick and easy to prepare and
decoration is often simple although you can get
carried away if you like!

You'll find recipes for old favorites such as
Chocolate Chip Muffins and Chocolate Chip
Cookies, Chocolate Butterfly Cakes and Sticky
Chocolate Brownies. There are also some new
cookies and small cakes to tickle your taste-buds, try
Chocolate & Coconut Squares or Malted Chocolate
Wedges. Finally, we have given the chocolate
treatment to some traditional recipes, turning them
into chocoholics delights – try Chocolate biscuits or
Chocolate Chip Flapjacks.

Chocolate Boxes

Makes 4

INGREDIENTS

8 ounces dark chocolate
8 ounces bought or ready-made
    plain or chocolate cake

2 tbsp apricot preserve
²/₃ cup heavy cream
1 tbsp maple syrup

prepared fresh fruit, such as small
    strawberries, raspberries, kiwi
    fruit, or red currants

1 Melt the dark chocolate and spread it evenly over a large sheet of baking parchment. Allow to harden in a cool room.

2 When just set, cut the chocolate into 2-inch squares and remove from the paper. Make sure that your hands are as cool as possible and handle the chocolate as little as possible.

3 Cut the cake into two 2-inch cubes, then cut each cube in half. Warm the apricot preserve and brush it over the sides of the cake

cubes. Carefully press a chocolate square onto each side of the cake cubes to make 4 chocolate boxes with cake at the bottom. Chill for 20 minutes.

4 Whip the heavy cream with the maple syrup until just holding its shape. Spoon or pipe a little of the mixture into each chocolate box.

5 Decorate the top of each box with the prepared fruit. If desired, the fruit can be partially dipped into melted

chocolate and allowed to harden before putting into the boxes.

COOK'S TIP

For the best results, keep the boxes well chilled and fill and decorate them just before you want to serve them.

Chocolate Cream Wraps

Makes 6-8

INGREDIENTS

2 eggs
4 tbsp superfine sugar

$^1/_3$ cup all-purpose flour
$1^1/_2$ tbsp unsweetened cocoa
4 tbsp apricot preserve

$^2/_3$ cup heavy cream, whipped
confectioners' sugar, to dust

1 Line 2 cookie sheets with pieces of baking parchment. Beat the eggs and sugar together until the mixture is very light and fluffy and the whisk leaves a trail when lifted.

2 Sift together the flour and unsweetened cocoa. Using a metal spoon or a spatula, gently fold it into the eggs and sugar in a figure eight movement.

3 Drop rounded table-spoons of the mixture onto the lined cookie sheets and spread them into oval shapes. Make sure they are well spaced, as they will spread during cooking.

4 Bake in a preheated oven at 425°F for about 6–8 minutes, or until springy to the touch. Leave the cakes on the cookie sheets to cool.

5 When cold, slide the cakes onto a damp dish cloth and set aside until cold. Carefully remove them from the dampened cloth. Spread the flat side of the cakes with apricot preserve, then spoon or pipe the whipped cream down the center of each one.

6 Fold the cakes in half and place them on a serving plate. Sprinkle them with a little confectioners' sugar and serve.

VARIATION

Fold 4 tsp of crème de menthe or 2 ounces melted chocolate into the cream for fabulous alternatives to plain cream wraps.

Small Cakes & Cookies

Chocolate Cupcakes with White Chocolate Frosting

Makes 18

INGREDIENTS

½ cup butter, softened	⅓ cup dark chocolate chips	FROSTING:
7 tbsp superfine sugar	1¼ cups self-rising flour	8 ounces white chocolate
2 eggs, lightly beaten	¼ cup unsweetened cocoa	5½ ounces low-fat cream cheese
2 tbsp milk		

1 Line an 18-hole muffin pan with individual paper cups.

2 Beat together the butter and sugar until pale and fluffy. Gradually add the eggs, beating well after each addition. Add a little of the flour if the mixture begins to curdle. Add the milk, then fold in the chocolate chips.

3 Sift together the flour and unsweetened cocoa

and fold into the mixture with a metal spoon or spatula. Divide the mixture equally between the paper cups and level the tops.

4 Bake in a preheated oven at 350°F for 20 minutes, or until well risen and springy to the touch. Transfer the cupcakes to a wire rack to cool.

5 To make the frosting, melt the chocolate, then let cool slightly.

Beat the cream cheese until softened and beat in the chocolate. Spread a little frosting over each cake and chill for 1 hour.

VARIATION

Add white chocolate chips or chopped pecans to the mixture instead of the dark chocolate chips, if you wish. You can also add the finely grated rind of 1 orange for a chocolate and orange flavor.

Chocolate Rum Babas

Makes 4

INGREDIENTS

³/₄ cup strong all-purpose flour
¹/₄ cup unsweetened cocoa
1 envelope active dry yeast
pinch of salt
1 tbsp superfine sugar
1¹/₂ ounces dark chocolate, grated
2 eggs

3 tbsp tepid milk
4 tbsp butter, melted

SYRUP:
4 tbsp clear honey
2 tbsp water
4 tbsp rum

TO SERVE:
whipped cream
unsweetened cocoa, to dust
fresh fruit (optional)

1 Lightly oil 4 individual ring pans. In a large warmed mixing bowl, sift the flour and unsweetened cocoa together. Stir in the yeast, salt, sugar, and grated chocolate. Beat the eggs, add the milk and butter, and beat until well mixed.

2 Make a well in the center of the dry ingredients and pour in the egg mixture, beating to mix to a batter. Beat for 10 minutes, ideally with an electric mixer with a dough hook. Divide the mixture between the pans – it should come halfway up the sides.

3 Place on a cookie sheet and cover with a damp dish cloth. Leave in a warm place until the mixture rises almost to the tops of the pans. Bake in a preheated oven at 400°F for 15 minutes.

4 To make the syrup, gently heat all the ingredients in a small pan. Turn out the babas and place on a rack placed above a tray to catch the syrup. Drizzle the syrup over the babas and leave for at least 2 hours for the syrup to soak in. Once or twice, spoon the syrup that has dripped onto the tray over the babas.

5 Fill the center of the babas with whipped cream and sprinkle a little unsweetened cocoa over the top. Serve the babas with fresh fruit, if desired.

No Bake Chocolate Squares

Makes 16

INGREDIENTS

9¹/₂ ounces dark chocolate
³/₄ cup butter
4 tbsp light corn syrup
2 tbsp dark rum (optional)

6 ounces plain cookies
¹/₃ cup toasted rice cereal
¹/₂ cup chopped walnuts or
    pecan nuts

¹/₂ cup candied cherries,
    roughly chopped
1 ounce white chocolate,
    to decorate

1 Place the dark chocolate in a double boiler with the butter, syrup, and rum, if using, over gently simmering water until melted, stirring continuously until blended.

2 Break the cookies into small pieces and stir into the chocolate mixture, along with the rice cereal, nuts, and cherries.

3 Line a 7-inch square cake pan with baking parchment. Pour the mixture into the pan and level the top, pressing down well with the back of a spoon.

Chill in the refrigerator for 2 hours.

4 To decorate, melt the white chocolate and drizzle it over the top of the cake in a random pattern. Let set. To serve, carefully turn out of the pan and remove the baking parchment. Cut the cake into 16 squares.

COOK'S TIP

Store in an airtight container in the refrigerator for up to 2 weeks.

VARIATIONS

For a coconut flavor, replace the rice cereal with shredded coconut and add a coconut-flavored liqueur.

VARIATIONS

Brandy or an orange-flavored liqueur can be used instead of the rum, if you wish. Cherry brandy also works well.

Chocolate Butterfly Cupcakes

Makes 12

INGREDIENTS

½ cup soft margarine
½ cup superfine sugar
2 large eggs
1¼ cups self-rising flour
2 tbsp unsweetened cocoa
1 ounce dark chocolate, melted

LEMON BUTTER CREAM:
½ cup sweet butter, softened
1⅓ cups confectioners' sugar, sifted
grated rind of ½ lemon
1 tbsp lemon juice
confectioners' sugar, to dust

1 Place 12 paper cups in a muffin pan. Place all the ingredients for the cakes, except the melted chocolate, in a large mixing bowl and beat with an electric mixer until the mixture is just smooth. Beat in the chocolate.

2 Spoon equal amounts of the cake mixture into each paper cup, filling them three-quarters full. Bake in a preheated oven at 350°F for 15 minutes, or until springy to the touch. Transfer the cakes to a wire rack and set aside to cool completely.

3 To make the lemon butter cream, place the butter in a mixing bowl and beat until fluffy, then gradually beat in the confectioners' sugar. Beat in the lemon rind and gradually add the lemon juice, beating well.

4 When cold, cut the top off each cupcake, using a serrated knife. Cut each top in half.

5 Spread or pipe the butter cream frosting over the cut surface of each cake and push the 2 cut pieces of cake top into the frosting to form wings. Sprinkle with confectioners' sugar.

VARIATION

For a chocolate butter cream, beat the butter and confectioners' sugar together, then beat in 1 ounce melted dark chocolate.

Sticky Chocolate Brownies

Makes 9

INGREDIENTS

$^1/_2$ cup sweet butter

$^3/_4$ cup superfine sugar

$^1/_2$ cup dark brown sugar

$4^1/_2$ ounces dark chocolate

1 tbsp light corn syrup

2 eggs

1 tsp chocolate or vanilla extract

$^3/_4$ cup all-purpose flour

2 tbsp unsweetened cocoa

$^1/_2$ tsp baking powder

1 Lightly grease and flour a shallow 8-inch square cake pan.

2 Place the butter, sugars, dark chocolate, and light corn syrup in a heavy-based saucepan and heat gently, stirring until the mixture is well blended and smooth. Remove from the heat and let cool.

3 Beat together the eggs and extract. Beat in the cooled chocolate mixture.

4 Sift together the flour, unsweetened cocoa, and baking powder and fold carefully into the egg and chocolate mixture, using a metal spoon or a spatula.

5 Spoon the mixture into the prepared pan and bake in a preheated oven at 350°F for 25 minutes, until the top is crisp and the edge of the cake is beginning to shrink away from the pan. The inside of the cake will still be quite dense and soft to the touch.

6 Allow the cake to cool completely in the

pan, then cut it into squares to serve.

VARIATION

This cake can be well wrapped and frozen for up to 2 months. Thaw at room temperature for about 2 hours or overnight in the refrigerator.

Chocolate Fudge Brownies

Makes 16

INGREDIENTS

7 ounces low-fat cream cheese
$^1/_2$ tsp vanilla extract
2 eggs
1$^1/_4$ cups superfine sugar

$^1/_2$ cup butter
3 tbsp unsweetened cocoa
$^3/_4$ cup self-rising flour, sifted
1$^3/_4$ ounces pecans, chopped

FUDGE FROSTING:
2 tbsp butter
1 tbsp milk
$^1/_2$ cup confectioners' sugar
2 tbsp unsweetened cocoa
pecans, to decorate (optional)

1 Lightly grease and flour a shallow 8-inch square cake pan.

2 Beat together the cheese, vanilla extract, and 5 tsp of the superfine sugar until smooth, then set aside.

3 Beat the eggs and remaining superfine sugar together until light and fluffy. Place the butter and unsweetened cocoa in a small saucepan and heat gently, stirring until the butter melts and the mixture combines, then stir it into the egg mixture. Fold in the flour and the chopped pecans, mixing well.

4 Pour half the brownie mixture into the pan and level the surface. Carefully spread the soft cheese over it, then cover it with the remaining brownie mixture. Bake in a preheated oven at 350°F for 40–45 minutes. Cool in the pan.

5 To make the frosting, melt the butter in the milk. Stir in the confectioners' sugar and unsweetened cocoa.

Spread the frosting over the brownies and decorate with pecans, if using. Let the frosting set, then cut the brownies into squares to serve.

VARIATION

Omit the cheese layer if preferred. Use walnuts in place of pecans.

Chocolate Chip Muffins

Makes 12

INGREDIENTS

$^1/_2$ cup soft margarine

1 cup superfine sugar

2 large eggs

$^2/_3$ cup full-fat unsweetened yogurt

5 tbsp milk

2 cups all-purpose flour

1 tsp baking soda

6 ounces dark chocolate chips

1 Line a muffin pan with 12 paper cups.

2 Place the margarine and sugar in a large mixing bowl and beat with a wooden spoon until light and fluffy. Beat in the eggs, yogurt, and milk until combined.

3 Sift the flour and baking soda together and add to the mixture. Stir until just blended.

4 Stir in the chocolate chips, then spoon the mixture into the paper cups, and bake in a preheated oven at 375°F for 25 minutes, or until a toothpick inserted into the center comes out clean. Cool the muffins in the pan for 5 minutes, then turn them out onto a wire rack to cool completely.

VARIATION

For chocolate and orange muffins, add the grated rind of 1 orange and replace the milk with fresh orange juice.

VARIATION

The mixture can also be used to make 6 large or 24 mini muffins. Bake mini muffins for 10 minutes, or until springy to the touch.

Chocolate Biscuits

Makes 9

INGREDIENTS

2 cups self-rising flour, sifted
1/4 cup butter
1 tbsp superfine sugar

1/3 cup chocolate chips
about 2/3 cup milk

1 Lightly grease a cookie sheet. Place the flour in a mixing bowl. Cut the butter into small pieces and rub it into the flour with your fingertips until the biscuit mixture resembles fine bread crumbs.

2 Stir in the superfine sugar and chocolate chips.

3 Mix in enough milk to form a soft dough.

4 On a lightly floured surface, roll out the dough to form a rectangle 4 × 6 inches, about 1 inch thick. Cut the dough into 9 squares.

5 Place the biscuits on the prepared cookie sheet, spacing them well apart.

6 Brush with a little milk and bake in a preheated oven at 425°F for 10–12 minutes, until the biscuits are risen and golden. Let cool slightly and serve warm

COOK'S TIP

To be at their best, all biscuits should be freshly baked and served warm. Split the warm biscuits and spread them with a little chocolate and hazelnut spread or a spoon of whipped cream.

VARIATION

Use dark, milk, or white chocolate chips or a mixture of all three. Use a 2-inch cookie cutter to cut out round biscuits, if preferred.

Pain au Chocolate

Makes 12

INGREDIENTS

4 cups strong all-purpose flour	1 egg, beaten lightly	3¹/₂ ounces dark chocolate, broken
¹/₂ tsp salt	1 cup tepid water	into 12 squares
1 envelope active dry yeast	³/₄ cup butter, softened	beaten egg, to glaze
2 tbsp white vegetable shortening		confectioners' sugar, to dust

1 Lightly grease a cookie sheet. Sift the flour and salt into a mixing bowl and stir in the yeast. Rub in the shortening with your fingertips. Add the egg and enough of the water to mix to a soft dough. Knead it for about 10 minutes to make a smooth elastic dough.

2 Roll out to form a rectangle 15 × 8 inches. Divide the butter into 3 portions and dot one portion over two-thirds of the rectangle, leaving a small border around the edge.

3 Fold the rectangle into 3 by first folding the plain part of the dough over and then the other side. Seal the edges of the dough by pressing with a rolling pin. Give the dough a quarter turn so the sealed edges are at the top and bottom. Re-roll and fold (without adding butter), then wrap the dough, and chill for 30 minutes.

4 Repeat steps 2 and 3 until all the butter has been used, chilling the dough each time. Re-roll and fold twice more without butter. Chill for a final 30 minutes.

5 Roll the dough to a rectangle 18 × 12 inches, trim and cut in half lengthwise. Cut each half into 6 rectangles and brush with beaten egg. Place a chocolate square at one end of each rectangle and roll up to form a sausage. Press the ends together and place, seam side down, on the cookie sheet. Cover and set aside to rise for 40 minutes in a warm place. Brush with beaten egg to glaze and bake in a preheated oven at 425°F for 20–25 minutes, until golden. Cool on a wire rack. Serve warm or cold.

Choc-Chip Tartlets

Makes 6

INGREDIENTS

1½ cups toasted hazelnuts
1¾ cups all-purpose flour
1 tbsp confectioners' sugar
⅓ cup soft margarine

FILLING:
2 tbsp cornstarch
1 tbsp unsweetened cocoa
1 tbsp superfine sugar
1¼ cups low-fat milk

3 tbsp chocolate and hazelnut
    spread
2½ tbsp dark chocolate chips
2½ tbsp milk chocolate chips
2½ tbsp white chocolate chips

1 Finely chop the nuts in a food processor. Add the flour, sugar, and margarine. Process for a few seconds, until the mixture resembles breadcrumbs. Add 2–3 tbsp water and process to form a soft dough. Cover and chill in the freezer for 10 minutes.

2 Roll out the dough and use it to line six 4-inch tartlet pans. Prick the bases with a fork and line them with loosely crumpled foil. Bake in a preheated oven at 400°F for 15 minutes. Remove and discard the foil

and bake for a further 5 minutes, until the pie shells are crisp and golden. Remove from the oven and set aside to cool.

3 Mix together the cornstarch, unsweetened cocoa, and sugar with enough milk to make a smooth paste. Stir in the remaining milk. Pour into a pan and cook gently over a low heat, stirring until thickened and smooth. Stir in the chocolate and hazelnut spread.

4 Mix together the chocolate chips and reserve a quarter. Stir half the remaining chips into the custard. Cover with damp wax paper and leave until almost cold, then stir in the second half of the chocolate chips. Spoon the mixture into the pie shells and set aside to cool. Decorate with the reserved chips, scattering them over the top.

Chocolate Eclairs

Makes about 10

INGREDIENTS

CHOUX PASTRY:
$^2/_3$ cup water
$^1/_4$ cup butter, cut into small pieces
$^3/_4$ cup strong all-purpose
    flour, sifted
2 eggs

PATISSERIE CREAM:
2 eggs, lightly beaten
4 tbsp superfine sugar
2 tbsp cornstarch
$1^1/_4$ cups milk
$^1/_4$ tsp vanilla extract

FROSTING:
2 tbsp butter
1 tbsp milk
1 tbsp unsweetened cocoa
$^1/_2$ cup confectioners' sugar
a little white chocolate, melted

1 Lightly grease a cookie sheet. Place the water in a saucepan, add the butter, and heat gently until the butter melts. Bring to a rolling boil, then remove the pan from the heat, and add the flour all at once, beating constantly until the mixture leaves the sides of the pan and forms a ball. Let cool slightly, then gradually beat in the eggs to form a smooth, glossy mixture. Spoon the mixture into a large pastry bag fitted with a $^1/_2$-inch plain tip.

2 Sprinkle the cookie sheet with a little water. Pipe éclairs 3 inches long, spaced well apart. Bake in a preheated oven at 400°F for 30–35 minutes, or until crisp and golden. Make a small slit in each one to let the steam escape. Cool on a rack.

3 To make the patisserie cream, beat the eggs and sugar until thick and creamy, then fold in the cornstarch. Heat the milk until almost boiling and pour into the eggs, beating constantly.

Transfer to the pan and cook over a low heat, stirring until thick. Remove the pan from the heat and stir in the vanilla extract. Cover with baking parchment and cool. To make the frosting, melt the butter with the milk in a pan, remove from the heat, and stir in the cocoa and sugar. Split the éclairs lengthwise and pipe in the patisserie cream. Spread the frosting over the top of the éclairs. Spoon the white chocolate on top, swirl it in, and let set.

Chocolate Orange Cookies

Makes about 30

INGREDIENTS

$^1/_3$ cup butter, softened	1 tbsp milk	FROSTING:
$^1/_3$ cup superfine sugar	2 cups all-purpose flour	1 cup confectioners' sugar, sifted
1 egg	$^1/_4$ cup unsweetened cocoa	3 tbsp orange juice
		a little dark chocolate, melted

1 Line 2 cookie sheets with baking parchment.

2 Beat together the butter and sugar until light and fluffy. Beat the egg and milk into the mixture until well combined. Sift together the flour and unsweetened cocoa and gradually mix together to form a soft dough. Use your fingers to incorporate the last of the flour and bring the dough together.

3 Roll out the dough on a lightly floured surface until ¼-inch thick. Using a 2-inch fluted round cutter, cut out as many cookies as you can. Re-roll the dough trimmings and cut out more cookies.

4 Place the cookies on the prepared cookie sheet, spaced apart, and bake in a preheated oven at 350°F for 10–12 minutes, or until golden.

5 Cool the cookies on the cookie sheet for a few minutes, then transfer to a wire rack to cool completely.

6 To make the frosting, place the confectioners' sugar in a bowl and stir in enough orange juice to form a thin frosting that will coat the back of a spoon. Spread the frosting over the cookies and let set. Drizzle with melted chocolate. Allow the chocolate to set before serving.

Chocolate Caramel Squares

Makes 16

INGREDIENTS

⅓ cup soft margarine
4 tbsp light brown sugar
1 cup all-purpose flour
½ cup rolled oats

CARAMEL FILLING:
2 tbsp butter
2 tbsp light brown sugar
7 ounce can condensed milk

TOPPING:
3½ ounces dark chocolate
1 ounce white chocolate (optional)

1 Beat together the margarine and brown sugar in a bowl until light and fluffy. Beat in the flour and the rolled oats. Use your fingertips to bring the mixture together, if necessary.

2 Press the mixture into the base of a shallow 8-inch square cake pan.

3 Bake in a preheated oven at 350°F for about 25 minutes, or until just golden and firm. Cool in the pan.

4 Place the ingredients for the caramel filling in a pan and heat gently, stirring until the sugar has dissolved and the ingredients combine. Bring to a boil over a very low heat, then boil very gently for 3-4 minutes, stirring constantly until thickened.

5 Pour the caramel filling over the cookie base in the pan and let set.

6 Melt the dark chocolate and spread it over the caramel. If using the white chocolate, melt it and pipe lines of white chocolate over the dark chocolate. Using a toothpick, feather the white chocolate into the dark chocolate. Let set completely. Cut into squares to serve.

COOK'S TIP

If desired, you can line the pan with baking parchment so that the cookie can be lifted out before cutting into pieces.

Chocolate Meringues

Makes 8

INGREDIENTS
---

4 egg whites
1 cup superfine sugar
1 tsp cornstarch
1¹/₂ ounces dark chocolate, grated

TO COMPLETE:
3¹/₂ ounces dark chocolate
²/₃ cup heavy cream

1 tbsp confectioners' sugar
1 tbsp brandy (optional)

---

1 Line 2 cookie sheets with baking parchment. Beat the egg whites until they are standing in soft peaks, then gradually beat in half the superfine sugar. Continue beating until the mixture is very stiff and glossy.

2 Carefully fold in the remaining sugar, the cornstarch, and grated chocolate with a metal spoon or spatula.

3 Spoon the mixture into a pastry bag fitted with a large star or plain tip. Pipe 16 large rosettes or mounds on the lined cookie sheets.

4 Bake in a preheated oven at 275°F for about 1 hour, changing the position of the cookie sheets halfway through cooking. Without opening the oven door, turn off the oven, and leave the meringues to cool in the oven. Once cold, carefully peel away the baking parchment.

5 Melt the dark chocolate and spread it over the base of the meringues. Stand them upside down on a wire rack until the chocolate has set. Whip the heavy cream together with confectioners' sugar and brandy (if using),

until the cream holds its shape. Spoon into a pastry bag and use to sandwich the meringues together in pairs. Serve.

VARIATION

To make mini meringues, use a star shaped tip and pipe about 24 small rosettes. Bake for about 40 minutes, until crisp.

Chocolate & Hazelnut Palmiers

Makes about 26

INGREDIENTS

13 ounces ready-made puff pastry dough	8 tbsp chocolate hazelnut spread $^1/_2$ cup chopped toasted hazelnuts	5 tsp superfine sugar

1 Lightly grease a cookie sheet. On a lightly floured surface, roll out the puff pastry dough to a rectangle about 15 × 9 inches in size.

2 Spread the chocolate hazelnut spread over the dough using a spatula, then scatter the chopped hazelnuts over the top.

3 Roll up one long side of the dough to the center, then roll up the other side so that they meet in the center. Where the pieces meet, dampen the edges with a little water to join them. Using a sharp knife, cut into thin slices.

Place each slice onto the prepared cookie sheet and flatten slightly with a spatula. Sprinkle the slices with the superfine sugar.

4 Bake in a preheated oven at 425°F, for about 10–15 minutes, until golden. Transfer to a wire rack to cool.

VARIATION

For an extra chocolate flavor, dip the palmiers in melted dark chocolate to half-cover each cookie.

COOK'S TIP

Palmiers can be served cold, but they are also delicious served warm.

The cookies can be frozen for up to 3 months in a sealed container.

Chocolate & Coconut Squares

Makes 9

INGREDIENTS

8 ounces dark chocolate
    graham crackers
$^1/_3$ cup butter or margarine
6 ounce can evaporated milk

1 egg, beaten
1 tsp vanilla extract
5 tsp superfine sugar
$^1/_3$ cup self-rising flour, sifted

1$^1/_4$ cups shredded coconut
1$^3/_4$ ounces dark chocolate
    (optional)

1 Grease a shallow 8-inch square cake pan and line the base with baking parchment.

2 Put the crackers in a plastic bag and crush them with a rolling pin or process them in a food processor.

3 Melt the butter or margarine in a saucepan and stir in the crushed crackers until well combined.

4 Press the mixture into the base of the cake pan.

5 Beat together the evaporated milk, egg, vanilla extract, and sugar until smooth. Stir in the flour and shredded coconut. Pour the mixture over the cracker base and level the top.

6 Bake in a preheated oven at 375°F for 30 minutes, or until the coconut topping is firm and just golden.

7 Cool in the cake pan for about 5 minutes, then cut into squares. Allow to cool completely in the pan.

8 Carefully remove the squares from the pan and place them on a board. Melt the dark chocolate (if using) and drizzle it over the squares to decorate them. Let the chocolate set before serving.

COOK'S TIP

Store the squares in an airtight container for up to 4 days. They can be frozen, undecorated, for up to 2 months. Thaw at room temperature.

Chocolate & Coconut Cookies

Makes about 24

INGREDIENTS

¹/₃ cup soft margarine

1 tsp vanilla extract

6 tbsp confectioners' sugar, sifted

1 cup all-purpose flour

2 tbsp unsweetened cocoa

²/₃ cup shredded coconut

2 tbsp butter

3¹/₂ ounces white marshmallows

¹/₄ cup shredded coconut

a little dark chocolate, melted

1 Lightly grease a cookie sheet. Beat together the margarine, vanilla extract, and confectioners' sugar in a mixing bowl until light and fluffy. Sift together the flour and unsweetened cocoa and beat into the mixture, together with the coconut.

2 Roll heaping teaspoons of the mixture into balls between your palms and place on the prepared cookie sheet, allowing room for the cookies to spread during cooking.

3 Flatten the balls slightly and bake in a preheated oven at 350°F for 12–15 minutes, until the cookies are just firm.

4 Leave the cookies to cool on the cookie sheet for a few minutes before transferring to a wire rack to cool completely.

5 Combine the butter and marshmallows in a small saucepan and heat gently, stirring until melted and well combined. Spread a little of the frosting mixture over each cookie and dip in

the coconut. Let set. Decorate the cookies with a little melted chocolate and let set completely before serving.

COOK'S TIP

Store these cookies in an airtight container for about 1 week. Alternatively, they can be frozen, undecorated, for up to 2 months.

Chocolate Crispy Bites

Makes 16

INGREDIENTS

WHITE LAYER:
4 tbsp butter
1 tbsp light corn syrup
5 1/2 ounces white chocolate
1/2 cup toasted rice cereal

DARK LAYER:
4 tbsp butter
2 tbsp light corn syrup

4 1/2 ounces dark chocolate, broken
into small pieces
3/4 cup toasted rice cereal

---

1 Lightly grease an 8-inch square cake pan and line with baking parchment.

2 To make the white chocolate layer, melt the butter, light corn syrup, and chocolate in a double boiler.

3 Remove from the heat and stir in the rice cereal until it is well combined.

4 Press into the prepared pan and level the surface of the mixture.

5 To make the dark chocolate layer, melt the butter, light corn syrup, and dark chocolate in a double boiler.

6 Remove from the heat and stir in the rice cereal until it is well coated. Pour the dark chocolate layer over the hardened white chocolate layer and refrigerate until the top layer has hardened.

7 Turn out of the cake pan and cut into small, evenly sized squares, using a sharp knife.

COOK'S TIP

These bites can be made up to 4 days ahead. Keep them covered in the refrigerator until ready to use.

Dutch Macaroons

Makes about 20

INGREDIENTS

rice paper
2 egg whites

1 cup superfine sugar
1½ cups ground almonds

8 ounces dark chocolate

1 Cover 2 cookie sheets with rice paper. Beat the egg whites in a large mixing bowl until stiff, then fold in the sugar and ground almonds.

2 Place the mixture in a large pastry bag fitted with a ½-inch plain tip and pipe fingers, about 3 inches long, allowing space for the mixture to spread during cooking.

3 Bake in a preheated oven at 350°F for 15–20 minutes, until golden. Transfer to a wire rack and let cool. Remove the excess rice paper from around the edges of the cookies.

4 Melt the chocolate and dip the base of each cookie into the chocolate. Place the macaroons on a sheet of baking parchment and allow to set.

5 Drizzle any remaining chocolate over the top of the cookies. Set completely before serving.

COOK'S TIP

Rice paper is edible so you can break off the excess from around the edge of the cookie. Remove it completely before dipping in the chocolate, if you prefer.

VARIATION

Almonds are most commonly used in macaroons, but they can be made with other ground nuts, such as hazelnuts.

Chocolate Chip Oatmeal Bars

Makes 12

INGREDIENTS

¹/₂ cup butter	1 tbsp light corn syrup	¹/₂ cup dark chocolate chips
¹/₃ cup superfine sugar	4 cups rolled oats	¹/₃ cup golden raisins

1 Lightly grease a shallow 8-inch square cake pan.

2 Place the butter, superfine sugar, and light corn syrup in a saucepan and cook over a low heat, stirring constantly, until the butter and sugar have melted and the mixture is well combined.

3 Remove the pan from the heat and stir in the rolled oats with a wooden spoon until they are well coated. Add the chocolate chips and the golden raisins and mix well to combine all the ingredients thoroughly.

4 Turn into the prepared pan and press down well.

5 Bake in a preheated oven at 350°F for 30 minutes. Cool slightly, then mark into bars or squares. When almost cold cut into bars or squares and transfer to a wire rack until cold.

COOK'S TIP

The bars will keep in an airtight container for up to 1 week, but they are so delicious they are unlikely to last that long!

VARIATION

Replace some of the oats with chopped nuts or sunflower seeds and a littleextra dried fruit. extra dried fruit.

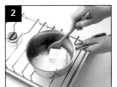

Chocolate Chip Cookies

Makes about 18

INGREDIENTS

$^1/_2$ cup soft margarine	$^1/_2$ tsp vanilla extract	1 tsp baking powder
$^1/_3$ cup light brown sugar	1 egg	$^2/_3$ cup dark chocolate chips
$^1/_4$ cup superfine sugar	$1^1/_2$ cups all-purpose flour	

---

1 Lightly grease 2 cookie sheets.

2 Place all of the ingredients in a large mixing bowl in the order listed and beat until well combined.

3 Place tablespoonfuls of the mixture onto the prepared cookie sheets, spacing them well apart to allow for spreading during cooking.

4 Bake in a preheated oven at 375°F for 10–12 minutes, or until the cookies are golden brown.

5 Using a spatula, transfer the cookies to a wire rack to cool completely.

VARIATIONS

For Choc & Nut Cookies, add $^1/_2$ cup chopped hazelnuts to the basic mixture.

For Double Choc Cookies, beat in $1^1/_2$ ounces melted dark chocolate.

VARIATIONS

For White Chocolate Chip Cookies, use white chocolate chips instead of the dark chocolate chips.

For Mixed Chocolate Chip Cookies, use a mixture of dark, milk, and white chocolate chips in the basic mixture.

For Chocolate Chip & Coconut Cookies, add $^1/_3$ cup shredded coconut to the basic mixture.

For Chocolate Chip & Raisin Cookies, add 5 tbsp raisins to the basic mixture.

Chocolate Shortbread

Makes 12

INGREDIENTS

4 tbsp superfine sugar
²/₃ cup butter, softened

1¹/₂ cups all-purpose flour
1 tbsp unsweetened cocoa

1³/₄ ounces dark chocolate,
finely chopped

1 Lightly grease a cookie sheet.

2 Place all the ingredients in a large mixing bowl in the order listed and beat together until they form a dough. Knead the dough lightly.

3 Place the dough on the cookie sheet and roll or press out to form an 8-inch round.

4 Pinch the edges of the dough with your fingertips to form a decorative edge. Prick the dough all over with a fork and mark into 12 wedges, using a sharp knife.

5 Bake in a preheated oven at 325°F for 40 minutes, until firm and golden. Cool slightly before cutting into wedges. Transfer to a wire rack to cool completely.

VARIATION

The shortbread dough can be pressed into a floured shortbread mold and turned out onto the cookie sheet before baking.

VARIATION

For round shortbread cookies, roll out the dough on a lightly floured surface to ¼ inch thick. Cut out 3-inch rounds with a cookie cutter. Transfer to a greased cookie sheet and bake as above. If desired, coat half the cookie in melted chocolate.

Malted Chocolate Wedges

Makes 16

INGREDIENTS

7 tbsp butter
2 tbsp light corn syrup
2 tbsp malted chocolate drink

8 ounces malted milk cookies
2³/4 ounces milk or dark chocolate,
    broken into pieces

2 tbsp confectioners' sugar
2 tbsp milk

1 Grease a shallow 7-inch round cake pan or flan pan and line the base.

2 Place the butter, light corn syrup, and malted chocolate drink in a small pan and heat gently, stirring all the time until the butter has melted and the mixture is well combined.

3 Crush the cookies in a plastic bag with a rolling pin, or process them in a food processor until they form crumbs. Stir the crumbs into the chocolate mixture and mix well.

4 Press the mixture into the prepared pan and chill in the refrigerator until firm.

5 Heat the chocolate pieces in a double boiler with the confectioners' sugar and the milk. Stir until the chocolate melts and the mixture is thoroughly combined.

6 Spread the chocolate frosting over the cookie base and allow to set in the pan. Using a sharp knife, cut into wedges to serve.

VARIATION

Add chopped pecan nuts to the cookie crumb mixture in step 3, if desired.

Chocolate Checkerboard Cookies

Makes about 18

INGREDIENTS

³/₄ cup butter, softened
6 tbsp confectioners' sugar
1 teaspoon vanilla extract or grated
   rind of ¹/₂ orange

2¹/₄ cups all-purpose flour
1 ounce dark chocolate, melted
a little beaten egg white

1 Lightly grease a cookie sheet. Beat the butter and confectioners' sugar in a mixing bowl until light and fluffy, then beat in the vanilla extract or the grated orange rind.

2 Gradually beat in the flour to form a soft dough. Use your fingers to incorporate the last of the flour and to bring the dough together.

3 Divide the dough into 2 equal pieces and beat the melted chocolate into one half. Keeping each half of the dough separate, cover and chill in the refrigerator for about 30 minutes.

4 Roll out each piece of dough to a rectangle about 3 x 8 inches long and 1¹/₂ inches thick. Brush one piece of dough with a little egg white and place the other piece of dough on top.

5 Cut the block of dough in half lengthwise and turn over one half. Brush the side of one strip with egg white and butt the other up to it, so that it resembles a checkerboard.

6 Cut the block into thin slices and place each slice flat on the cookie sheet, allowing enough room for them to spread a little during cooking.

7 Bake in a preheated oven at 350°F for about 10 minutes, until just firm. Cool on the cookie sheets for a few minutes before carefully transferring to a wire rack with a spatula. Cool completely.

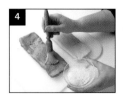

Viennese Chocolate Fingers

Makes about 18

INGREDIENTS

¹/₂ cup sweet butter
6 tbsp confectioners' sugar
1¹/₂ cups self-rising flour, sifted

3 tbsp cornstarch
7 ounces dark chocolate

1 Lightly grease 2 cookie sheets. Beat the butter and sugar together in a mixing bowl until light and fluffy. Gradually beat the flour and cornstarch into the mixture.

2 Melt 2³/₄ ounces of the dark chocolate and beat into the cookie dough.

3 Place in a pastry bag fitted with a large star tip and pipe fingers about 2 inches long on the prepared cookie sheets, slightly spaced apart to allow for spreading during cooking.

4 Bake in a preheated oven at 375°F for 12–15 minutes. Cool slightly on the cookie sheets, then carefully transfer with a spatula to a wire rack and let cool completely.

5 Melt the remaining dark chocolate and dip one end of each cookie in the chocolate, allowing the excess to drip back into the bowl.

6 Place the cookies on a sheet of baking parchment and allow to completely set before serving.

COOK'S TIP

If the cookie dough is too thick to pipe, beat in a little milk to thin it out.

VARIATION

Dip the base of each cookie in melted chocolate and allow to set. Sandwich the cookies together in pairs with a little butter cream.

Chocolate Pretzels

Makes about 30

INGREDIENTS

¹/₂ cup sweet butter	TO FINISH:
7 tbsp superfine sugar	1 tbsp butter
1 egg	3¹/₂ ounces dark chocolate
2 cups all-purpose flour	confectioners' sugar, to dust
¹/₄ cup unsweetened cocoa	

1 Lightly grease a cookie sheet. Beat together the butter and sugar in a mixing bowl until light and fluffy. Beat in the egg.

2 Sift together the flour and unsweetened cocoa and gradually beat in to form a soft dough. Use your fingers to incorporate the last of the flour and bring the dough together. Chill for 15 minutes.

3 Break small pieces from the dough and roll them into thin sausage shapes about 4 inches long

and ¹/₄-inch thick. Twist into pretzel shapes by first making a circle and then twisting the ends through to make the shape of a letter "B."

4 Place the pretzels on the prepared cookie sheet, slightly spaced apart to allow room for spreading during cooking.

5 Bake in a preheated oven at 375°F for 8–12 minutes. Allow the pretzels to cool slightly on the cookie sheet, then transfer to a wire rack to cool completely.

6 Melt the butter and chocolate in a double boiler, stirring to combine.

7 Dip half of each pretzel into the chocolate and allow the excess chocolate to drip back into the bowl. Place the pretzels on a sheet of baking parchment and allow to set.

8 When set, dust the non-chocolate coated side of each pretzel with confectioners' sugar before serving.

Chocolate Wheat Cookies

Makes about 20

INGREDIENTS

¹/₃ cup butter	1 cup whole-wheat self-rising flour
7 tbsp raw crystal sugar	¹/₂ cup self-rising flour, sifted
1 egg	4¹/₂ ounces chocolate
1 ounce wheatgerm	

1 Lightly grease a cookie sheet. Beat the butter and sugar until fluffy. Add the egg and beat well. Stir in the wheatgerm and flours. Bring the mixture together with your hands.

2 Roll heaping teaspoons of the mixture into balls and place on the prepared cookie sheet, allowing room for the cookies to spread during cooking.

3 Flatten the cookies slightly with a fork. Bake in a preheated oven at 350°F for 15–20 minutes, until golden. Cool on the cookie sheet for a few minutes before transferring the cookies to a wire rack to cool completely.

4 Melt the chocolate, then dip each cookie in the chocolate to cover the base and come a little way up the sides. Let the excess drip back into the bowl.

5 Place the cookies, chocolate side up, on a sheet of baking parchment and allow to set in a cool place before serving.

COOK'S TIP

These cookies can be frozen very successfully. Freeze them at the end of step 3 for up to 3 months. Thaw and then dip them in melted chocolate.

Hot Desserts

Chocolate is comforting at anytime but no more so
than when served in a steaming hot pudding. It is
hard to think of anything more warming,
comforting and homely than tucking into a steamed
hot Chocolate Fudge Pudding or a Hot Chocolate
Soufflé. The child in us will love the chocolate
addition to nursery favourites such as Chocolate
Bread & Butter Pudding. In fact, there are several
old favourites that have been given the chocolate
treatment, bringing them bang up to date and
putting them on the chocolate lovers map.

When you are feeling in need of something a little
more sophisticated, try the new-style Chocolate
Apple Pancake Stack, or Chocolate Pear &
Almond Flan, which might be more in keeping. Or
try Chocolate Zabaglione for a sophisticated creamy,
warm dessert set to get your taste buds in a whirl!

This chapter is packed full of chocolate
delights, with different tastes and textures to add
warmth to any day.

Chocolate Queen of Puddings

Serves 4

INGREDIENTS

1³/₄ ounces dark chocolate
2 cups chocolate-flavored milk
1³/₄ cups fresh white or whole-
  wheat breadcrumbs

¹/₂ cup superfine sugar
2 eggs, separated
4 tbsp black cherry preserve

1 Break the chocolate into small pieces and place in a saucepan with the chocolate-flavored milk. Heat gently, stirring until the chocolate melts. Bring almost to a boil, then remove the pan from the heat.

2 Place the breadcrumbs in a large mixing bowl with 5 tsp of the superfine sugar. Pour the chocolate milk over the breadcrumb mixture and mix well. Beat in the egg yolks.

3 Spoon into a 5-cup pie dish and bake in a preheated oven at 350°F for 25–30 minutes, or until set and firm to the touch.

4 Beat the egg whites in a large grease-free bowl until standing in soft peaks. Gradually beat in the remaining superfine sugar and continue beating until you have a glossy, thick meringue.

5 Spread the black cherry preserve over the surface of the chocolate mixture and pile or pipe the meringue on top. Return the pudding to the oven for about 15 minutes, or until the meringue is crisp and golden.

VARIATION

If you wish, add ¹/₂ cup shredded coconut to the breadcrumbs and omit the preserve.

Chocolate Eve's Pudding with Bitter Chocolate Sauce

Serves 4

INGREDIENTS

1¼ cups fresh or frozen raspberries, thawed if frozen
2 eating apples
4 tbsp seedless raspberry preserve
2 tbsp port (optional)

SPONGE TOPPING:
4 tbsp soft margarine
4 tbsp superfine sugar
⅔ cup self-rising flour, sifted
1¾ ounces white chocolate, grated
1 egg
2 tbsp milk

BITTER CHOCOLATE SAUCE:
3 ounces dark chocolate, broken into small pieces
⅔ cup light cream

1 Peel, core, and thickly slice the apples. Place the slices of apple and the raspberries in a shallow 5-cup ovenproof dish.

2 Place the raspberry preserve and port (if using) in a small pan and heat gently until the preserve melts and combines thoroughly with the port. Remove from the heat and pour the mixture over the fruit.

3 Place the margarine, sugar, flour, grated white chocolate, egg, and milk in a large mixing bowl and beat well until the mixture is smooth.

4 Spoon the sponge mixture over the fruit and level the surface. Bake in a preheated oven at 350°F for 40–45 minutes, or until the sponge is golden and springy to the touch.

5 To make the sauce, place the chocolate in a heavy-based saucepan with the cream. Heat gently, beating until smooth. Serve warm with the dessert.

VARIATION

Use dark chocolate in the sponge and top with apricot halves, covered with peach schnapps and apricot conserve.

Mini Chocolate Ginger Puddings with Chocolate Custard

Serves 4

INGREDIENTS

1/2 cup soft margarine	2 eggs	CHOCOLATE CUSTARD:
3/4 cup self-rising flour, sifted	1/4 cup unsweetened cocoa, sifted	2 egg yolks
7 tbsp superfine sugar	1 ounce dark chocolate	1 tbsp superfine sugar
	1 3/4 ounces preserved ginger	1 tbsp cornstarch
		1 1/4 cups milk
		3 1/2 ounces dark chocolate, broken into pieces
		confectioners' sugar, to dust

1 Lightly grease 4 individual heatproof bowls. Place the margarine, flour, sugar, eggs, and unsweetened cocoa in a mixing bowl and beat until well combined and smooth. Chop the chocolate and ginger and stir into the mixture.

2 Spoon the cake mixture into the prepared bowls and level the top. The mixture should three-quarters fill the bowls. Cover the bowls with baking parchment and cover with a pleated sheet of foil. Steam for 45 minutes, until the puddings are cooked and springy to the touch.

3 Meanwhile, make the custard. Beat together the egg yolks, sugar, and cornstarch to form a smooth paste. Heat the milk until boiling and pour it over the egg mixture. Return to the pan and cook over a very low heat, stirring until thick. Remove from the heat and beat in the chocolate. Stir until the chocolate melts.

4 Lift the puddings from the steamer, run a knife around them, and turn out onto serving plates. Dust with sugar and drizzle with some chocolate custard. Serve the remaining custard separately.

Chocolate Bread & Butter Pudding

Serves 4

INGREDIENTS

8 ounces brioche	2 egg yolks
1 tbsp butter	4 tbsp superfine sugar
1³/₄ ounces dark chocolate chips	15 ounce can light evaporated milk
1 egg	

1 Cut the brioche into thin slices. Lightly butter one side of each slice.

2 Place a layer of brioche, buttered side down, in the bottom of a shallow ovenproof dish. Sprinkle a few chocolate chips over the top.

3 Continue layering the brioche and chocolate chips, finishing with a layer of bread on top.

4 Beat together the egg, egg yolks, and sugar until well combined. Heat the milk in a small saucepan until it just begins to simmer.

Gradually add it to the egg mixture, beating well.

5 Pour the custard over the pudding and let stand for 5 minutes. Press the brioche down into the milk.

6 Place in a roasting pan and fill with boiling water to come halfway up the side of the dish (this is known as a *bain-marie*).

7 Bake in a preheated oven at 350°F for 30 minutes, or until the custard has set. Let cool for 5 minutes before serving. Alternatively, serve cold.

VARIATION

For a double-chocolate pudding, heat the milk with 1 tbsp of unsweetened cocoa, stirring until well dissolved, then continue from step 4.

Chocolate French Toasties

Serves 4–6

INGREDIENTS

1³/₄ ounces dark chocolate	2 tbsp rum (optional)	3 tbsp superfine sugar
²/₃ cup milk	8 thick slices white bread	a little whipped cream, to serve
1 egg	butter or oil, for frying	
4 tbsp seedless raspberry preserve	¹/₂ tsp ground cinnamon	

1 Break the chocolate into small pieces and place in a small pan with the milk. Heat gently, stirring until the chocolate melts. Let cool slightly.

2 Beat the egg in a large mixing bowl and beat in the warm chocolate milk.

3 Heat the raspberry preserve gently and stir in the rum, if using. Set aside and keep warm.

4 Remove the crusts from the bread, cut into triangles, and dip each one into the chocolate mixture. Heat the butter or oil in a skillet and fry the bread triangles for 2–3 minutes, until just crispy, turning once.

5 Mix together the cinnamon and superfine sugar and sprinkle it over the toast. Serve with the hot preserve sauce and a little whipped cream.

COOK'S TIP

Young children adore this dessert. Cut the bread into fingers to make it easier for them to handle.

VARIATION

If you wish, try this recipe using brioche or fruit bread for a tasty variation.

Chocolate Fudge Pudding

Serves 6

INGREDIENTS

³/₄ cup soft margarine
1 ¹/₄ cups self-rising flour
¹/₂ cup light corn syrup
3 eggs
¹/₄ cup unsweetened cocoa

CHOCOLATE FUDGE SAUCE:
3 ¹/₂ ounces dark chocolate
¹/₂ cup sweetened condensed milk
4 tbsp heavy cream

1 Lightly grease a 5-cup heatproof bowl.

2 Place the ingredients for the sponge in a mixing bowl and beat until well combined and smooth.

3 Spoon into the prepared bowl and level the top. Cover with baking parchment and tie a pleated sheet of foil over the bowl. Steam for 1½–2 hours, until the pudding is cooked and springy to the touch.

4 To make the sauce, break the chocolate into small pieces and place in a small pan with the condensed milk. Heat gently, stirring until the chocolate melts.

5 Remove the pan from the heat and stir in the heavy cream, mixing well.

6 To serve the pudding, turn it out onto a serving plate and pour over a little of the chocolate fudge sauce. Serve the remaining sauce separately.

COOK'S TIP

To cook the dessert in the microwave, cook it, uncovered, on high for 4 minutes, turning the bowl once. Let stand for at least 5 minutes before turning out. While the pudding is standing, make the sauce. Break the chocolate into pieces and place in a microwave-safe bowl with the milk. Cook on high for 1 minute, then stir until the chocolate melts. Stir in the heavy cream and serve.

Chocolate Fruit Crumble

Serves 4

INGREDIENTS

14 ounce can apricots, in
  natural juice
1 pound cooking apples, peeled and
  thickly sliced
³/₄ cup all-purpose flour

¹/₃ cup butter
²/₃ cup dried oats
4 tbsp superfine sugar
²/₃ cup chocolate chips

1 Lightly grease an ovenproof dish with a little butter or margarine.

2 Drain the apricots, reserving 4 tbsp of the juice. Place the apples and apricots in the prepared ovenproof dish with the reserved apricot juice and toss to mix.

3 Sift the flour into a mixing bowl. Cut the butter into small cubes and rub it in with your fingertips until the mixture resembles fine breadcrumbs. Stir in the dried oats, sugar, and chocolate chips.

4 Sprinkle the crumble mixture over the apples and apricots and level the top roughly. Do not press the crumble into the fruit.

5 Bake in a preheated oven at 350°F for 40–45 minutes, or until the topping is golden. Serve hot or cold.

COOK'S TIP

You can use dark, milk, or white chocolate chips in this recipe or a mixture of all three.

VARIATION

For a double chocolate crumble, replace 1–2 tablespoons of flour with unsweetened cocoa.

VARIATION

Other fruits can be used to make this crumble – fresh pears mixed with fresh or frozen raspberries work well. If you do not use canned fruit, add 4 tablespoons of orange juice to the fresh fruit.

Poached Pears with Mascarpone Chocolate Sauce

Serves 6

INGREDIENTS

6 firm ripe pears	rind of 1 orange	CHOCOLATE SAUCE:
7 tbsp superfine sugar	2 cloves	6 ounces dark chocolate
2 cinnamon sticks	1 bottle rosé wine	1¼ cups mascarpone cheese
		2 tbsp orange-flavored liqueur

1 Carefully peel the pears, leaving the stalk intact.

2 Place the sugar, cinnamon sticks, orange rind, cloves, and wine in a saucepan that will hold the 6 pears snugly.

3 Heat gently until the sugar has dissolved, then add the pears to the liquid, and bring to a simmer. Cover and poach gently for 20 minutes. If serving them cold, leave the pears to cool in the liquid, then chill until required. If serving hot, leave the pears in the hot liquid while preparing the chocolate sauce.

4 To make the sauce, melt the chocolate. Beat together the cheese and the orange-flavored liqueur. Beat the cheese mixture into the chocolate.

5 Remove the pears from the poaching liquid and place on a serving plate. Add a generous spoonful of sauce on the side and serve the remainder separately.

COOK'S TIP

There is no need to waste the tasty poaching liquid. Boil it rapidly in a clean pan for about 10 minutes to reduce to a syrup. Use the syrup to sweeten a fresh fruit salad or spoon it over ice cream.

COOK'S TIP

Rosettes of cream can be piped onto the dessert, if desired.

Saucy Chocolate Pudding

Serves 4

INGREDIENTS

1¼ cups milk	½ cup butter	FOR THE SAUCE:
2¾ ounces dark chocolate	1¼ cups self-rising flour	3 tbsp unsweetened cocoa
½ tsp vanilla extract	2 tbsp unsweetened cocoa	4 tbsp light brown sugar
1 cup 1 tbsp superfine sugar	confectioners' sugar, to dust	1¼ cups boiling water

1 Lightly grease a 3¾-cup ovenproof dish.

2 Place the milk in a small pan. Break the chocolate into pieces and add to the milk. Heat gently, stirring until the chocolate melts. Let cool slightly. Stir in the vanilla extract.

3 Beat together the superfine sugar and butter in a bowl until light and fluffy. Sift the flour and unsweetened cocoa together. Add to the bowl with the chocolate milk and beat until smooth, using an electric beater if you have one. Pour the mixture into the prepared dish.

4 To make the sauce, mix together the unsweetened cocoa and sugar. Add a little boiling water and mix to a smooth paste, then stir in the remaining water. Pour the sauce over the pudding, but do not mix in.

5 Place the dish on a cookie sheet and bake in a preheated oven at 350°F for 40 minutes, or until dry on top and springy to the touch. Let stand for about 5 minutes, then dust with a little confectioners' sugar just before serving.

VARIATION

For a mocha sauce, add 1 tbsp instant coffee to the cocoa and sugar in step 4, before mixing to a paste with boiling water.

Pecan & Chocolate Fudge Ring

Serves 6

INGREDIENTS

FUDGE SAUCE:
3 tbsp butter
3 tbsp light brown sugar
4 tbsp light corn syrup

2 tbsp milk
1 tbsp unsweetened cocoa
1½ ounces dark chocolate
½ cup finely chopped pecans

CAKE:
½ cup soft margarine
7 tbsp light brown sugar
1 cup self-rising flour
2 eggs
2 tbsp milk
1 tbsp light corn syrup

1 Lightly grease an 8-inch ring pan.

2 To make the fudge sauce, place the butter, sugar, syrup, milk, and unsweetened cocoa in a small pan and heat gently, stirring until combined.

3 Break the chocolate into pieces, add to the mixture, and stir until melted. Stir in the chopped nuts. Pour into the base of the pan and set aside to cool.

4 To make the cake, place all the ingredients in a mixing bowl and beat until smooth. Carefully spoon the cake mixture over the chocolate fudge sauce.

5 Bake in a preheated oven at 350°F for 35 minutes, or until the cake is cooked through and springy to the touch.

6 Cool in the pan for 5 minutes, then turn out on to a serving dish and serve.

COOK'S TIP

To make in the microwave, place the butter, sugar, syrup, milk, and unsweetened cocoa for the sauce in a microwave-safe bowl. Cook on high for 2 minutes, stirring twice. Stir in the chocolate until melted, then add the nuts. Pour into a 5-cup microwave-safe ring mold. Make the cake and cook on high for 3–4 minutes, until just dry on top; let stand for 5 minutes.

Chocolate Meringue Pie

Serves 6

INGREDIENTS

8 ounces dark chocolate
    graham crackers
4 tbsp butter

FILLING:
3 egg yolks
4 tbsp superfine sugar
4 tbsp cornstarch
2 1/2 cups milk
3 1/2 ounces dark chocolate, melted

MERINGUE:
2 egg whites
7 tbsp superfine sugar
1/4 tsp vanilla extract

1 Place the graham crackers in a plastic bag and crush with a rolling pin. Pour into a mixing bowl. Melt the butter and stir it into the cracker crumbs until well mixed. Press the cookie mixture firmly into the base and up the sides of a 9-inch flan pan or dish.

2 To make the filling, beat the egg yolks, superfine sugar, and cornstarch in a large bowl until they form a smooth paste, adding a little of the milk if necessary. Heat the milk until almost boiling, then slowly pour it into the egg mixture, constantly beating well.

3 Return the mixture to the saucepan and cook gently, beating constantly, until it thickens. Remove from the heat. Beat in the melted chocolate, then pour it onto the graham cracker base.

4 To make the meringue, beat the egg whites in a large mixing bowl until standing in soft peaks. Gradually beat in about two-thirds of the sugar until the mixture is stiff and glossy. Fold in the remaining sugar and the vanilla extract.

5 Spread the meringue over the filling, covering it completely and swirling the surface with the back of a spoon to give it an attractive finish. Bake in the center of a preheated oven at 375°F for about 30 minutes, or until the meringue is golden. Serve hot or just warm.

Chocolate Apple Pie

Serves 6

INGREDIENTS

CHOCOLATE PIE CRUST:

4 tbsp unsweetened cocoa

$1^3/_4$ cups all-purpose flour

2 egg yolks

$^1/_2$ cup softened butter

4 tbsp superfine sugar

few drops of vanilla extract

cold water, to mix

FILLING:

1 pound 10 ounces cooking apples

2 tbsp butter

$^1/_2$ tsp ground cinnamon

$^3/_4$ cup dark chocolate chips

a little egg white, beaten

$^1/_2$ tsp superfine sugar

whipped cream or vanilla ice cream,
  to serve

1 To make the crust, sift the unsweetened cocoa and flour into a mixing bowl and rub in the butter until the mixture resembles fine breadcrumbs. Stir in the sugar. Add the egg yolk, vanilla extract, and enough water to mix to a dough.

2 Roll out the dough on a lightly floured surface and use to line a deep 8-inch flan or cake pan. Chill for 30 minutes. Roll out any trimmings and cut out some pastry leaves to decorate the top of the pie.

3 Peel, core, and thickly slice the apples. Place half the slices in a saucepan with the butter and cinnamon and cook over a gentle heat, stirring occasionally, until the apples soften.

4 Stir in the uncooked apple slices, let cool slightly, then stir in the chocolate chips. Prick the base of the pie shell with a fork and pile the apple mixture into it. Arrange the pastry leaves decoratively on top. Brush the leaves with a little egg white and

sprinkle with superfine sugar.

5 Bake in a preheated oven at 350°F for 35 minutes, until the pastry is golden and crisp. Serve warm or cold, with whipped cream or vanilla ice cream.

Chocolate Pear & Almond Flan

Serves 6

INGREDIENTS

³/₄ cup all-purpose flour
¹/₄ cup ground almonds
¹/₄ cup margarine
about 3 tbsp water

FILLING:
14 ounce can pear halves, in
    natural juice
4 tbsp butter
4 tbsp superfine sugar
2 eggs, beaten
1 cup ground almonds
2 tbsp unsweetened cocoa
few drops of almond extract
confectioners' sugar, to dust

CHOCOLATE SAUCE:
4 tbsp superfine sugar
3 tbsp light corn syrup
¹/₃ cup water
6 ounces dark chocolate, broken
    into pieces
2 tbsp butter

1 Lightly grease an 8-inch flan pan. Sift the flour into a mixing bowl and stir in the almonds. Rub in the margarine with your fingertips until the mixture resembles breadcrumbs. Add enough water to mix to a soft dough. Cover, chill in the freezer for 10 minutes, then roll out, and use to line the pan. Prick the base and chill.

2 To make the filling, drain the pears well. Beat the butter and sugar until light and fluffy. Beat in the eggs. Fold in the almonds, unsweetened cocoa, and extract. Spread the chocolate mixture in the pie shell and arrange the pears on top, pressing down lightly. Bake in the center of a preheated oven at 400°F for 30 minutes, or until the filling has risen.

Cool slightly and transfer to a serving dish, if preferred. Dust with sugar.

3 To make the sauce, place the sugar, syrup, and water in a pan and heat gently, stirring until the sugar dissolves. Boil gently for 1 minute. Remove the pan from the heat, add the chocolate and butter, and stir until melted. Serve with the flan.

Chocolate & Banana Crêpes

Serves 4

INGREDIENTS

3 large bananas	HOT CHOCOLATE SAUCE:	CRÊPES:
6 tbsp orange juice	1 tbsp unsweetened cocoa	1 cup all-purpose flour
grated rind of 1 orange	2 tsp cornstarch	1 tbsp unsweetened cocoa
2 tbsp orange- or banana-flavored liqueur	3 tbsp milk	1 egg
	1½ ounces dark chocolate	1 tsp sunflower oil
	1 tbsp butter	1¼ cups milk
	½ cup light corn syrup	oil, for frying
	¼ tsp vanilla extract	

1 Peel and slice the bananas and arrange them in a dish with the orange juice and rind and the liqueur. Set aside.

2 Mix the unsweetened cocoa and cornstarch in a bowl, then stir in the milk. Break the dark chocolate into pieces and place in a pan with the butter and light corn syrup. Heat gently, stirring until well blended. Add the cocoa mixture and bring to a boil over a gentle heat, stirring. Simmer for 1 minute, then remove from the heat and stir in the vanilla extract.

3 To make the crêpes, sift the flour and cocoa into a mixing bowl and make a well in the center. Add the egg and oil. Gradually beat in the milk to form a smooth batter. Heat a little oil in a heavy-based skillet and pour off any excess. Pour in a little batter and tilt the pan to coat the base. Cook over a medium heat until the underside is browned. Flip over and cook the other side. Slide the crêpe out of the pan and keep warm. Repeat until all the batter has been used.

4 To serve, reheat the chocolate sauce for 1-2 minutes. Fill the crêpes with the bananas and fold in half or into triangles. Pour a little chocolate sauce on top and serve.

Chocolate Apple Pancake Stack

Serves 4–6

INGREDIENTS

2 cups all-purpose flour
1½ tsp baking powder
4 tbsp superfine sugar
1 egg

1 tbsp butter, melted
1¼ cups milk
1 eating apple
⅓ cup dark chocolate chips

Hot Chocolate Sauce (see page 160)
or maple syrup, to serve

1 Sift the flour and baking powder into a mixing bowl. Stir in the superfine sugar. Make a well in the center and add the egg and melted butter. Gradually beat in the milk and continue beating to form a smooth batter.

2 Peel, core, and grate the apple and stir it into the batter with the chocolate chips.

3 Heat a griddle or heavy-based skillet over a medium heat and grease it lightly. For each pancake, place about 2 tablespoons of

the batter onto the griddle or skillet and spread to make a 3-inch round.

4 Cook for a few minutes, until you see bubbles appear on the surface of the pancake. Turn over and cook for a further 1 minute. Remove from the pan and keep warm. Repeat with the remaining batter to make about 12 pancakes.

5 To serve, stack 2 or 3 pancakes on an individual serving plate and serve with the hot chocolate sauce or maple syrup.

COOK'S TIP

To keep the cooked pancakes warm, pile them on top of each other with baking parchment in between to prevent them from sticking to each other.

VARIATION

Milk chocolate chips can be used instead of the dark ones, if preferred.

Chocolate Fondue

Serves 6–8

INGREDIENTS

CHOCOLATE FONDUE:
8 ounces dark chocolate
³/₄ cup heavy cream
2 tbsp brandy

TO SERVE:
selection of fruit
white and pink marshmallows
sweet cookies

1 Break the chocolate into small pieces and place in a small saucepan, together with the heavy cream.

2 Heat the mixture gently, stirring constantly, until the chocolate has melted and blended with the cream.

3 Remove the pan from the heat and stir in the brandy.

4 Pour into a fondue pot or a small flameproof dish and keep warm, preferably over a small burner.

5 Serve with a selection of fruit, marshmallows, and cookies for dipping. The fruit and marshmallows can be spiked on fondue forks, wooden skewers, or ordinary forks for dipping into the chocolate fondue.

COOK'S TIP

To prepare the fruit for dipping, cut larger fruit into bite-size pieces. Fruit that discolors, such as bananas, apples, and pears, should be dipped in a little lemon juice as soon as it is cut.

COOK'S TIP

It is not essential to use a special fondue set. Dish warmers that use a night light are just as good for keeping the fondue warm. If you do not have one, stand the fondue dish in a larger dish and pour in enough boiling water to come halfway up the fondue dish. Whichever method you use to keep your fondue warm, place it on a heatproof stand to protect the table.

Hot Chocolate Soufflé

Serves 4

INGREDIENTS

3$\frac{1}{2}$ ounces dark chocolate
1$\frac{1}{4}$ cups milk
2 tbsp butter
4 large eggs, separated
1 tbsp cornstarch

4 tbsp superfine sugar
$\frac{1}{2}$ tsp vanilla extract
$\frac{2}{3}$ cup dark chocolate chips
superfine and confectioners' sugar,
    to dust

CHOCOLATE CUSTARD:
2 tbsp cornstarch
1 tbsp superfine sugar
2 cups milk
1$\frac{3}{4}$ ounces dark chocolate

1 Grease a 5-cup soufflé dish and sprinkle with superfine sugar. Break the chocolate into small pieces.

2 Heat the milk with the butter in a pan until almost boiling. Mix the egg yolks, cornstarch, and superfine sugar in a bowl and pour in some of the hot milk, beating. Return the mixture to the pan and cook gently, stirring constantly, until thickened. Add the chocolate and stir until melted. Remove the pan from the heat and stir in the extract.

3 Beat the egg whites until standing in soft peaks. Fold half the egg whites into the chocolate mixture. Fold in the rest with the chocolate chips. Pour into the dish and bake in a preheated oven at 350°F for 40–45 minutes, until well risen.

4 Meanwhile, make the custard. Put the cornstarch and sugar in a small bowl and mix to a smooth paste with a little of the milk. Heat the remaining milk until almost boiling. Pour a little of the hot milk

into the cornstarch, mix well, then pour it back into the pan. Cook gently, stirring, until thickened. Break the chocolate into pieces and add to the custard, stirring until melted.

5 Dust the soufflé with sugar and serve immediately with the chocolate custard.

Chocolate Zabaglione

Serves 2

INGREDIENTS

4 egg yolks
4 tbsp superfine sugar
1¾ ounces dark chocolate

1 cup Marsala
unsweetened cocoa, to dust

1 Using an electric handmixer beat together the egg yolks and superfine sugar in a large glass mixing bowl until you have a very pale mixture.

2 Grate the chocolate finely and fold it into the egg mixture. Fold in the Marsala.

3 Place the mixing bowl over a saucepan of gently simmering water and set the mixer on the lowest speed. Cook gently, beating continuously, until the mixture thickens; take care not to overcook or the mixture will curdle.

4 Spoon the hot mixture into warm individual glass dishes and dust lightly with unsweetened cocoa. Serve the zabaglione as soon as possible while it is warm, light, and fluffy.

COOK'S TIP

Spoon the zabaglione into coffee cups and serve with amaretti cookies to the side of the saucer.

COOK'S TIP

Make the dessert just before serving, as the mixture will separate if left to stand. If it begins to curdle, you may be able to save it if you remove it from the heat immediately and place it in a bowl of cold water to stop the cooking. Beat vigorously until the mixture comes together.

Cold Desserts

Cool, creamy, sumptuous, indulgent
are just a few of the words that spring to mind
when you think of cold chocolate desserts.
The desserts contained in this chapter are a
combination of all of these.

Some of the desserts are surprisingly quick and
simple to make, while others are more elaborate.
One of the best things about these desserts is they
can all be made in advance, some times days in
advance, making them perfect for entertaining. A
quick decoration when necessary is all that is needed
on the day. Even the Baked Chocolate Alaska can
be assembled in advance and popped into the
oven just before serving.

Chocolate Mint Swirl

Serves 6

INGREDIENTS

1¼ cups heavy cream
⅔ cup creamy fromage frais or
   thick unsweetened yogurt

2 tbsp confectioners' sugar
1 tbsp crème de menthe
6 ounces dark chocolate

chocolate, to decorate

1 Place the cream in a large mixing bowl and beat until standing in soft peaks.

2 Fold in the fromage frais or yogurt and sugar, then place about one-third of the mixture in a smaller bowl. Stir the crème de menthe into the smaller bowl. Melt the dark chocolate and stir it into the remaining mixture.

3 Place alternate spoonfuls of the 2 mixtures into serving glasses, then swirl the mixture together to give a decorative effect. Chill until required.

4 To make the piped chocolate decorations, melt a small amount of chocolate and place in a paper pastry bag.

5 Place a sheet of baking parchment on a board and pipe squiggles, stars, or flower shapes with the melted chocolate. Alternatively, to make curved decorations, pipe decorations onto a long strip of baking parchment, then carefully place the strip over a rolling pin, securing with tape. Allow the chocolate to set, then carefully remove from the baking parchment.

6 Decorate each dessert with piped chocolate decorations and serve. The desserts can be decorated and then chilled, if desired.

COOK'S TIP

Pipe the patterns freehand or draw patterns onto baking parchment first, turn the parchment over, and then pipe the chocolate, following the drawn outline.

Chocolate Rum Pots

Serves 6

INGREDIENTS

8 ounces dark chocolate	4 tbsp dark rum	TO DECORATE:
4 eggs, separated	4 tbsp heavy cream	a little whipped cream
⅓ cup superfine sugar		chocolate shapes (see page 176)

1 Melt the chocolate and let cool slightly.

2 Beat the egg yolks with the superfine sugar in a bowl until very pale and fluffy; this will take about 5 minutes with an electric mixer.

3 Drizzle the chocolate into the mixture and fold it in, together with the rum and the heavy cream.

4 Beat the egg whites in a grease-free bowl until standing in soft peaks. Fold the egg whites into the chocolate mixture in 2 batches. Divide the mixture between 6 custard pots or other individual dishes, and chill for at least 2 hours.

5 To serve, decorate with a little whipped cream and small chocolate shapes.

VARIATION

These delicious little pots can be flavored with brandy instead of rum, if desired.

COOK'S TIP

Make sure you use a perfectly clean and grease-free bowl for beating the egg whites. They will not aerate if any grease is present, as the smallest amount breaks down the bubbles in the whites, preventing them from trapping and holding air.

Chocolate & Vanilla Creams

Serves 4

INGREDIENTS

2 cups heavy cream	2 tsp gelatin	MARBLED CHOCOLATE SHAPES:
1/3 cup superfine sugar	3 tbsp water	a little melted white chocolate
1 vanilla bean	1 3/4 ounces dark chocolate	a little melted dark chocolate
3/4 cup crème fraîche or sour cream		

1 Place the cream and sugar in a saucepan. Cut the vanilla bean into 2 pieces and add to the cream. Heat gently, stirring, until the sugar has dissolved, then bring to a boil. Reduce the heat and simmer for 2–3 minutes.

2 Remove the pan from the heat and take out the vanilla bean. Stir in the crème fraîche or sour cream.

3 Sprinkle the gelatin over the water in a small heatproof bowl and allow to become spongy, then place over a pan of hot water and stir until dissolved. Stir into the cream mixture. Pour half of this mixture into another mixing bowl.

4 Melt the dark chocolate and stir it into one half of the cream mixture. Pour the chocolate mixture into 4 glass serving dishes and chill for 15–20 minutes, until just set. Keep the vanilla mixture at room temperature.

5 Spoon the vanilla mixture on top of the chocolate mixture and chill until the vanilla is set.

6 Meanwhile, make the shapes for the decoration. Spoon the melted white chocolate into a paper pastry bag and snip off the tip. Spread some melted dark chocolate on a piece of baking parchment. While still wet, pipe a fine line of white chocolate in a scribble over the top. Use the tip of a toothpick to marble the white chocolate into the dark. When firm but not too hard, cut into shapes with a small shaped cutter or a sharp knife. Chill the shapes until firm, then use to decorate the desserts before serving.

Chocolate Hazelnut Pots

Serves 6

INGREDIENTS

2 eggs
2 egg yolks
1 tbsp superfine sugar
1 tsp cornstarch
2¹/₂ cups milk

3 ounces dark chocolate
4 tbsp chocolate and hazelnut
   spread

TO DECORATE:
grated chocolate or large chocolate
   curls (see page 66)

1 Beat together the eggs, egg yolks, superfine sugar, and cornstarch until thoroughly combined. Heat the milk until almost boiling.

2 Gradually pour the milk into the eggs, beating as you do so. Melt the chocolate and hazelnut spread in a double boiler, then beat the melted chocolate mixture into the eggs.

3 Pour into 6 small ovenproof dishes and cover the dishes with foil. Place them in a roasting pan. Fill the pan with boiling water to come halfway up the sides of the dishes.

4 Bake in a preheated oven at 325°F for 35–40 minutes, until the custard is just set. Remove from the pan and cool, then chill until required. Serve decorated with grated chocolate or chocolate curls.

COOK'S TIP

This dish is traditionally made in little pots called pots de crème, *which are individual ovenproof dishes with a lid. Custard pots are fine. The dessert can also be made in one large dish; cook for about 1 hour or until set.*

COOK'S TIP

The foil lid prevents a skin from forming on the surface of the custards.

Mocha Creams

Serves 4

INGREDIENTS

8 ounces dark chocolate
1 tbsp instant coffee
1¼ cups boiling water
1 envelope gelatin

3 tbsp cold water
1 tsp vanilla extract
1 tbsp coffee-flavored
   liqueur (optional)

1¼ cups heavy cream
4 chocolate coffee beans
8 amaretti cookies

1 Break the chocolate into small pieces and place in a saucepan with the coffee. Stir in the boiling water and heat gently, stirring, until the chocolate melts.

2 Sprinkle the gelatin over the cold water and allow it to become spongy, then beat it into the hot chocolate mixture to dissolve it.

3 Stir in the vanilla extract and coffee-flavored liqueur, if using. Let cool until it begins to thicken; beat from time to time.

4 Beat the cream until it forms soft peaks, then reserve a little for decorating the desserts, and fold the remainder into the chocolate mixture. Spoon into serving dishes and allow to set.

5 Decorate with the reserved cream and coffee beans and serve with the cookies.

COOK'S TIP

If desired, the dessert can be made in one large serving dish.

VARIATION

To add a delicious almond flavor to the dessert, replace the coffee-flavored liqueur with almond-flavored liqueur.

Layered Chocolate Mousse

Serves 8

INGREDIENTS

3 eggs	3 tbsp water	chocolate caraque, to decorate (see
1 tsp cornstarch	1¼ cups heavy cream	page 208)
4 tbsp superfine sugar	2¾ ounces dark chocolate	
1¼ cups milk	2¾ ounces white chocolate	
1 envelope gelatin	2¾ ounces milk chocolate	

1 Line a 1-pound loaf pan with baking parchment. Separate the eggs, putting each egg white in a separate bowl. Place the egg yolks and sugar in a large mixing bowl and beat until well combined. Place the milk in a pan and heat gently, stirring, until almost boiling. Pour the milk into the egg yolks, beating.

2 Set the bowl over a pan of gently simmering water and cook, stirring, until the mixture thickens enough to thinly coat the back of a wooden spoon.

3 Sprinkle the gelatin over the water in a small heatproof bowl and allow to become spongy. Place over a pan of hot water and stir until dissolved. Stir into the hot mixture. Set aside to cool.

4 Whip the cream until just holding its shape. Fold into the egg custard, then divide the mixture into 3. Melt the 3 types of chocolate separately. Fold the dark chocolate into one egg custard portion. Beat one egg white until standing in soft peaks and fold into the dark chocolate custard

until combined. Pour into the prepared pan and level the top. Chill in the coldest part of the refrigerator until just set. Leave the remaining mixtures at room temperature.

5 Fold the white chocolate into another portion of the egg custard. Beat another egg white and fold in. Pour on top of the dark chocolate layer and chill quickly. Repeat with the remaining milk chocolate and egg white. Chill until set. To serve, carefully turn out onto a serving dish and decorate with chocolate caraque.

Chocolate Marquise

Serves 6

INGREDIENTS

7 ounces dark chocolate	1 tsp chocolate extract or 1 tbsp	TO SERVE:
¹/₂ cup butter	chocolate-flavored liqueur	crème fraîche
3 egg yolks	1¹/₄ cups heavy cream	chocolate-dipped fruits
¹/₃ cup superfine sugar		(see page 64)
		unsweetened cocoa, to dust

1 Break the chocolate into pieces. Place the chocolate and butter in a double boiler and stir until melted and well combined. Remove from the heat and set aside to cool.

2 Place the egg yolks in a mixing bowl with the sugar and beat until the mixture becomes pale and fluffy. Using an electric beater on low speed, slowly beat in the cool chocolate mixture. Stir in the chocolate extract or chocolate-flavored liqueur.

3 Whip the cream until just holding its shape. Fold into the chocolate mixture. Spoon into 6 small custard pots or individual metal molds. Chill for at least 2 hours.

4 To serve, turn out the desserts onto individual serving dishes. If you have difficulty turning them out, dip the molds into a bowl of warm water for a few seconds to help the marquise to slip out. Serve with chocolate-dipped fruit and crème fraîche, and dust with unsweetened cocoa.

COOK'S TIP

The slight tartness of the crème fraîche contrasts well with this very rich dessert. Dip the fruit in white chocolate to give a good color contrast.

Iced White Chocolate Terrine

Serves 8–10

INGREDIENTS

2 tbsp sugar	10½ ounces white chocolate	1¼ cups heavy cream
5 tbsp water	3 eggs, separated	

1 Line a 1-pound loaf pan with aluminum foil or plastic wrap, pressing out as many creases as you can.

2 Place the sugar and water in a heavy-based pan and heat gently, stirring constantly, until the sugar has dissolved. Bring to a boil and boil for 1–2 minutes, until syrupy, then remove the pan from the heat.

3 Break the white chocolate into small pieces and stir it into the syrup, continuing to stir until the chocolate has melted and combined with the syrup. Set aside to cool slightly.

4 Beat the egg yolks into the chocolate mixture. Set aside to cool completely.

5 Lightly whip the cream until just holding its shape and fold it into the chocolate mixture.

6 Beat the egg whites in a grease-free bowl until they are standing in soft peaks. Fold into the chocolate mixture. Pour into the prepared loaf pan and freeze for 8 hours or overnight.

7 To serve, remove from the freezer about 10–15 minutes before serving. Turn out of the pan and cut into slices to serve.

COOK'S TIP

To make a coulis, place 8 ounces soft fruit of your choice – strawberries, black or red currants, mango, or raspberries are ideal – in a food processor or blender. Add 1–2 tbsp confectioners' sugar and blend to form a purée. If the fruit contains seeds, rub the purée through a strainer to remove them. Chill until required.

Chocolate Banana Sundae

Serves 4

INGREDIENTS

GLOSSY CHOCOLATE SAUCE:

2 ounces dark chocolate

4 tbsp light corn syrup

1 tbsp butter

1 tbsp brandy or rum (optional)

SUNDAE:

4 bananas

²/₃ cup heavy cream

8–12 scoops of good quality vanilla
  ice cream

³/₄ cup slivered or chopped
  almonds, toasted

grated or flaked chocolate,
  to sprinkle

4 fan wafer cookies

1 To make the chocolate sauce, break the chocolate into small pieces and place in a double boiler with the syrup and butter. Heat until melted, stirring until well combined. Remove the bowl from the heat and stir in the brandy or rum, if using.

2 Slice the bananas and whip the cream until just holding its shape. Place a scoop of ice cream in the bottom of 4 tall sundae dishes. Top with slices of banana, some chocolate sauce, a spoonful of cream, and a generous sprinkling of nuts.

3 Repeat the layers, finishing with a spoonful of cream, sprinkled with nuts and a little grated or flaked chocolate. Serve with fan wafer cookies.

VARIATION

Use half vanilla ice cream and half chocolate ice cream, if desired.

VARIATION

For a traditional banana split, halve the bananas lengthwise and place on a plate with two scoops of ice cream between. Top with cream and sprinkle with nuts. Serve with the glossy chocolate sauce poured over the top.

Rich Chocolate Ice Cream

Serves 6-8

INGREDIENTS

ICE CREAM:
1 egg
3 egg yolks
6 tbsp superfine sugar

1¼ cups milk
9 ounces dark chocolate
1¼ cups heavy cream

TRELLIS CUPS:
3½ ounces dark chocolate

1 Beat together the egg, egg yolks, and superfine sugar in a mixing bowl until thoroughly combined. Heat the milk until almost boiling.

2 Gradually pour the hot milk into the eggs, beating as you do so. Place the bowl over a pan of gently simmering water and cook, stirring, until the mixture thickens sufficiently to thinly coat the back of a wooden spoon.

3 Break the dark chocolate into small pieces and add to the hot mixture. Stir until the chocolate has melted. Cover with a sheet of dampened baking parchment and let cool.

4 Whip the cream until just holding its shape, then fold into the cooled chocolate mixture. Transfer to a freezer container and freeze for 1–2 hours, until the mixture is frozen 1 inch from the sides.

5 Scrape the ice cream into a chilled bowl and beat again until smooth. Re-freeze until firm.

6 To make the trellis cups, invert a muffin pan and cover 6 alternate mounds with plastic wrap. Melt the chocolate, place it in a paper pastry bag, and snip off the end.

7 Pipe a circle around the base of the mound, then pipe chocolate back and forth over it to form a trellis; carefully pipe a double thickness. Pipe around the base again. Chill until set, then lift from the pan, and remove the plastic wrap. Serve the ice cream in the trellis cups.

Baked Chocolate Alaska

Serves 6

INGREDIENTS

2 eggs	3 egg whites
4 tbsp superfine sugar	2/3 cup superfine sugar
6 tbsp all-purpose flour	4 1/2 cups good quality chocolate
2 tbsp unsweetened cocoa	ice cream

1 Grease a 7-inch round cake pan and line the base with baking parchment.

2 Beat the egg and the superfine sugar in a mixing bowl until very thick and pale. Sift the flour and unsweetened cocoa together and carefully fold into the egg mixture.

3 Pour into the prepared pan and bake in a preheated oven at 425°F for 7 minutes, or until springy to the touch. Transfer to a wire rack to cool completely.

4 Beat the egg whites in a grease-free bowl until they are standing in soft peaks. Gradually add the sugar, beating until you have a thick, glossy meringue.

5 Place the sponge cake on a cookie sheet and pile the ice cream onto the center heaping it up into a dome.

6 Pipe or spread the meringue over the ice cream, making sure the ice cream is completely enclosed. (At this point the dessert can be frozen, if desired.)

7 Return it to the oven, for 5 minutes, until the meringue is just golden. Serve immediately.

COOK'S TIP

This dessert is delicious served with a black currant coulis. Cook a few black currants in a little orange juice until soft, purée, and rub through a strainer. Sweeten to taste with a little confectioners' sugar.

White Chocolate Ice Cream in a Cookie Cup

Serves 6

INGREDIENTS

ICE CREAM:

1 egg
1 egg yolk
3 tbsp superfine sugar
5 1/2 ounces white chocolate
1 1/4 cups milk
2/3 cup heavy cream

COOKIE CUPS:

1 egg white
4 tbsp superfine sugar
2 tbsp all-purpose flour, sifted
2 tbsp unsweetened cocoa, sifted
2 tbsp butter, melted

1 Place baking parchment on 2 cookie sheets. To make the ice cream, beat the egg, egg yolks, and sugar. Break the chocolate into pieces and melt in a double boiler with 3 tbsp of the milk. Heat the milk until almost boiling and pour into the eggs, beating. Place over a pan of simmering water and cook, stirring, until the mixture thickens enough to coat the back of a wooden spoon. Beat in the chocolate. Cover with dampened baking parchment and cool.

2 Whip the cream until just holding its shape and fold into the custard. Transfer to a freezer container and freeze the mixture for 1–2 hours until frozen 1 inch from the sides. Scrape into a bowl and beat again until smooth. Re-freeze until firm.

3 To make the cups, beat the egg white and sugar together. Beat in the flour and cocoa, then the butter. Place 1 tbsp of mixture on one sheet and spread out to a 5-inch round. Bake in a preheated oven at 400°F for 4–5 minutes. Remove and mold over an upturned cup. Let set, then cool on a wire rack. Repeat to make 6 cups. Serve the ice cream in the cookie cups.

Chocolate Horns with Ginger Cardamom Cream

Serves 6

INGREDIENTS

1 egg white
4 tbsp superfine sugar
2 tbsp all-purpose flour
2 tbsp unsweetened cocoa
2 tbsp butter, melted
1³/₄ ounces dark chocolate

CARDAMOM CREAM:
²/₃ cup heavy cream
1 tbsp confectioners' sugar
¹/₄ tsp ground cardamom

pinch of ground ginger
1 ounce preserved ginger, finely
   chopped

1 Place a sheet of baking parchment on 2 cookie sheets. Lightly grease 6 cream horn molds. To make the horns, beat the egg white and sugar together in a mixing bowl until well combined. Sift the flour and unsweetened cocoa together, then beat into the egg, followed by the melted butter.

2 Place 1 tablespoon of the mixture on 1 cookie sheet and spread out to form a 5-inch round. Bake in a preheated oven at

400°F for 4–5 minutes.

3 Working quickly, remove the cookie with a spatula and wrap around the cream horn mold to form a cone. Allow to set, then remove from the mold. Repeat to make 6 cones.

4 Melt the chocolate and dip the open edges of the horn in the chocolate. Place on a piece of baking parchment and allow to set.

5 To make the cardamom cream, place the cream in a bowl and sift the confectioners' sugar and ground spices over the surface. Whip the cream until standing in soft peaks. Fold in the chopped ginger and use to fill the chocolate cones.

Chocolate Charlotte

Serves 8

INGREDIENTS

about 22 ladyfingers
4 tbsp orange-flavored liqueur
9 ounces dark chocolate
²/₃ cup heavy cream
4 eggs
²/₃ cup superfine sugar

TO DECORATE:
²/₃ cup heavy cream
2 tbsp superfine sugar
¹/₂ tsp vanilla extract
large dark chocolate curls,
(see page 66)

chocolate leaves (see page 44) or
chocolate shapes
(see page 176)

1 Line the base of a Charlotte mold or a deep 7-inch round cake pan with a piece of baking parchment.

2 Place the ladyfingers on a tray and sprinkle with half the orange-flavored liqueur. Use to line the sides of the mold or pan, trimming if necessary to make a tight fit.

3 Break the chocolate into small pieces and melt in a double boiler. Remove from the heat and stir in the heavy cream until well combined.

4 Separate the eggs and place the whites in a large grease-free bowl. Beat the egg yolks into the chocolate mixture.

5 Beat the egg whites until standing in stiff peaks, then gradually add the superfine sugar, beating until stiff and glossy. Carefully fold the egg whites into the chocolate mixture in 2 batches, taking care not to knock out all the air. Pour into the center of the mold. Trim the lady-fingers so that they are level with the chocolate mixture. Chill for at least 5 hours.

6 To decorate, beat the cream, sugar, and vanilla extract together until standing in soft peaks. Turn out the Charlotte onto a serving dish. Pipe cream rosettes around the base and decorate with chocolate curls and leaves.

Marble Cheesecake

Serves 10–12

INGREDIENTS

BASE:
2 cups toasted oatmeal
1/2 cup toasted hazelnuts, chopped
4 tbsp butter
1 ounce dark chocolate

FILLING:
12 ounces cream cheese
7 tbsp superfine sugar
3/4 cup thick unsweetened yogurt
1 1/4 cups heavy cream

1 envelope gelatin
3 tbsp water
6 ounces dark chocolate, melted
6 ounces white chocolate, melted

1 Place the toasted oatmeal in a plastic bag and crush with a rolling pin. Pour the crushed cereal into a mixing bowl and stir in the hazelnuts.

2 Melt the butter and chocolate together over a low heat and stir into the cereal mixture, stirring until well coated.

3 Using the bottom of a glass, press the mixture into the base and up the sides of an 8-inch springform pan.

4 Beat together the cheese and sugar with a wooden spoon until smooth. Beat in the yogurt. Whip the cream until just holding its shape and fold into the mixture. Sprinkle the gelatin over the water in a heatproof bowl and allow to become spongy. Place over a pan of hot water and stir until dissolved. Stir into the mixture.

5 Divide the mixture in half and beat the dark chocolate into one half and the white chocolate into the other half.

6 Place alternate spoonfuls of mixtures on top of the cereal base. Swirl the filling together with the tip of a knife to give a marbled effect. Level the top with a spatula. Chill in the refrigerator until set.

COOK'S TIP

For a lighter texture, fold in 2 egg whites beaten to soft peaks before folding in the cream in step 4.

Banana & Coconut Cheesecake

Serves 10

INGREDIENTS

8 ounces chocolate chip cookies	2 ripe bananas	TO DECORATE:
4 tbsp butter	4¹/₂ ounces dark chocolate	1 banana
1¹/₂ cups cream cheese	1 envelope gelatin	lemon juice
¹/₃ cup superfine sugar	3 tbsp water	a little melted chocolate
¹/₂ cup grated fresh coconut	²/₃ cup heavy cream	
2 tbsp coconut-flavored liqueur		

1 Place the cookies in a plastic bag and crush with a rolling pin. Pour into a mixing bowl. Melt the butter and stir it into the cookie crumbs until well coated. Firmly press the cookie mixture into the base and up the sides of an 8-inch springform pan.

2 Beat together the cheese and superfine sugar until well combined, then beat in the grated coconut and coconut-flavored liqueur. Mash the 2 bananas and beat them into the cheese mixture.

Melt the dark chocolate and beat it in until well combined.

3 Sprinkle the gelatin over the water in a heatproof bowl and allow to become spongy. Place over a pan of hot water and stir until dissolved. Stir into the chocolate mixture. Whip the cream until just holding its shape and stir it into the chocolate mixture. Spoon over the cookie base and chill until set.

4 To serve, carefully transfer to a serving plate. Slice the banana, toss in the lemon juice, and arrange around the edge of the cheesecake. Drizzle with melted chocolate and allow to set.

COOK'S TIP

To crack the coconut, pierce 2 of the "eyes" and drain off the liquid. Tap hard around the center with a hammer until it cracks; split apart.

Chocolate Brandy Torte

Serves 12

INGREDIENTS

BASE:

9 ounces ginger cookies

2³/₄ ounces dark chocolate

¹/₂ cup butter

FILLING:

8 ounces dark chocolate

1¹/₄ cups mascarpone cheese

2 eggs, separated

3 tbsp brandy

1¹/₄ cups heavy cream

4 tbsp superfine sugar

TO DECORATE:

¹/₂ cup heavy cream

chocolate coffee beans

1 Put the cookies in a plastic bag and crush with a rolling pin or crush in a food processor. Transfer to a bowl. Melt the chocolate and butter together and pour over the cookies. Mix well, then use to line the base and sides of a 9-inch loose-based fluted flan pan or springform pan. Chill while you are preparing the filling.

2 To make the filling, melt the dark chocolate in a pan, remove from the heat, and beat in the mascarpone cheese, egg yolks, and brandy.

3 Lightly whip the cream until just holding its shape and fold in the chocolate mixture.

4 Beat the egg whites in a grease-free bowl until standing in soft peaks. Add the superfine sugar a little at a time and beat until thick and glossy. Fold into the chocolate mixture, in 2 batches, until just mixed.

5 Spoon the mixture into the prepared base and chill for at least 2 hours. Carefully transfer to a serving plate. To decorate, whip the cream and pipe onto the cheesecake and add the chocolate coffee beans.

VARIATION

If chocolate coffee beans are unavailable, use chocolate-coated raisins to decorate.

Chocolate Shortcake Towers

Serves 6

INGREDIENTS

SHORTCAKE:

1 cup butter

$^{1}/_{2}$ cup light brown sugar

1$^{3}/_{4}$ ounces dark chocolate, grated

2$^{1}/_{2}$ cups all-purpose flour

TO FINISH:

2 cups fresh raspberries

2 tbsp confectioners' sugar

1$^{1}/_{4}$ cups heavy cream

3 tbsp milk

3 ounces white chocolate, melted

confectioners' sugar, to dust

1 Lightly grease a cookie sheet. To make the shortcake, beat together the butter and sugar until light and fluffy. Beat in the dark chocolate. Mix in the flour to form a stiff dough.

2 Roll out the dough on a lightly floured surface and stamp out eighteen 3-inch rounds with a fluted cookie cutter. Place the rounds on the cookie sheet and bake in a preheated oven at 400°F for 10 minutes, until crisp and golden. Cool on the cookie sheet.

3 To make the coulis, set aside about ½ cup of the raspberries. Put the remainder in a food processor together with the confectioners' sugar, and process to a purée. Rub through a strainer to remove the seeds. Chill. Set aside 2 teaspoons of the cream. Whip the remainder until just holding its shape. Fold in the milk and the melted chocolate.

4 For each tower, spoon a little coulis onto a serving plate. Drop small dots of the reserved cream into the coulis around the

edge of the plate and use a toothpick to drag through the cream to make a pattern.

5 Place a shortcake round on the plate and spoon on a little of the chocolate cream. Top with 2 or 3 raspberries, top with another shortcake and repeat. Place a third cake on top. Dust with sugar.

Black Forest Trifle

Serves 6–8

INGREDIENTS

6 thin slices chocolate butter cream roll	1¾ cups milk	TO DECORATE:
2 x 14 ounce cans black cherries	3 egg yolks	dark chocolate, melted
2 tbsp kirsch	1 egg	maraschino cherries (optional)
1 tbsp cornstarch	2¾ ounces dark chocolate	
2 tbsp superfine sugar	1¼ cups heavy cream, lightly whipped	

1 Place the slices of chocolate roll in the bottom of a glass serving bowl.

2 Drain the black cherries, reserving 6 tablespoons of the juice. Arrange the cherries on top of the layer of cake. Sprinkle with the reserved cherry juice and the kirsch.

3 In a bowl, mix the cornstarch and super-fine sugar. Stir in enough of the milk to mix to a smooth paste. Beat in the egg yolks and the whole egg.

4 Heat the remaining milk in a small saucepan until almost boiling, then gradually pour it into the egg mixture, beating well until it is combined.

5 Place the bowl over a pan of hot water and cook over a low heat, stirring constantly, until the custard thickens. Add the chocolate and stir until melted.

6 Pour the chocolate custard over the cherries and cool. When cold, spread the cream over the custard, swirling with the back of a spoon. Chill before decorating.

7 To make chocolate caraque, spread the melted dark chocolate on a marble or acrylic board. As it begins to set, pull a knife through the chocolate at a 45-degree angle, working quickly. Remove each caraque as you make it and chill firmly before using.

Champagne Mousse

Serves 4

INGREDIENTS

SPONGE:

4 eggs

7 tbsp superfine sugar

²/₃ cup self-rising flour

2 tbsp unsweetened cocoa

2 tbsp butter, melted

MOUSSE:

1 envelope gelatin

3 tbsp water

1¹/₄ cups Champagne

1¹/₄ cups heavy cream

2 egg whites

¹/₃ cup superfine sugar

TO DECORATE:

2 ounces dark chocolate, melted

fresh strawberries

1 Line a 15 × 10 inch jelly roll pan with greased baking parchment. Place the eggs and sugar in a bowl and beat with an electric mixer until the mixture is very thick and leaves a trail when lifted. Sift the flour and unsweetened cocoa together and fold into the egg mixture. Fold in the butter. Pour into the pan and bake in a preheated oven at 400°F for 8 minutes, or until springy to the touch. Cool for 5 minutes, then turn out onto a wire rack until cold. Line four 4-inch baking rings with baking parchment. Line the sides with 1-inch strips of cake and the bases with rounds.

2 To make the mousse, sprinkle the gelatin over the water and set aside until it is spongy. Place the bowl over a pan of hot water; stir until completely dissolved. Stir in the champagne.

3 Whip the cream until just holding its shape. Fold in the champagne mixture. Leave in a cool place, stirring occasionally, until on the point of setting. Beat the egg whites until the mixture stands in soft peaks, add the sugar and beat until glossy. Fold into the setting mixture. Spoon into the sponge cases, allowing the mixture to go above the sponge. Chill in the refrigerator for 2 hours. Pipe the melted chocolate in squiggles on a piece of parchment and let set. Decorate the mousses.

Chocolate Freezer Cake

Serves 8–10

INGREDIENTS

4 eggs	2¼ cups chocolate and mint
¾ cup superfine sugar	ice cream
¾ cup self-rising flour	Glossy Chocolate Sauce
3 tbsp unsweetened cocoa	(see page 188)

1 Lightly grease a 9-inch ring pan. Place the eggs and sugar in a large mixing bowl. Using an electric mixer if you have one, beat the mixture until it is very thick and the beater leaves a trail when lifted.

2 Sift together the flour and unsweetened cocoa and fold into the egg mixture. Pour into the prepared pan and bake in a preheated oven at 350°F for 30 minutes, or until springy to the touch. Cool in the pan before turning out onto a wire rack to cool completely.

3 Rinse the cake pan and line with a strip of plastic wrap, overhanging slightly. Cut the top off the cake about ½ inch thick and set aside.

4 Return the cake to the pan. Using a spoon, scoop out the center of the cake, leaving a shell about ½ inch thick.

5 Remove the ice cream from the freezer and let stand for a few minutes, then beat with a wooden spoon until softened a little. Fill the center of the cake with the ice cream, leveling the top. Replace the top of the cake.

6 Cover with the overhanging plastic wrap and freeze for at least 2 hours.

7 To serve, turn the cake out onto a serving dish and drizzle with some of the chocolate sauce in an attractive pattern, if you wish. Cut the cake into slices and serve the remaining sauce separately.

Mississippi Mud Pie

Serves 8–10

INGREDIENTS

2 cups all-purpose flour
1/4 cup unsweetened cocoa
2/3 cup butter
5 tsp superfine sugar
about 2 tbsp cold water

FILLING:
3/4 cup butter
12 ounces dark brown sugar
4 eggs, lightly beaten
4 tbsp unsweetened cocoa, sifted
5 1/2 ounces dark chocolate
1 1/4 cups light cream
1 tsp chocolate extract

TO DECORATE:
1 3/4 cups heavy cream, whipped
thick bar of chocolate

1 To make the dough, sift the flour and unsweetened cocoa together into a mixing bowl. Rub in the butter with your fingertips until the mixture resembles fine breadcrumbs. Stir in the sugar and just enough cold water to mix to a soft dough. Chill for about 15 minutes.

2 Roll out the dough on a lightly floured surface and use to line a deep 9-inch loose-based flan pan or ceramic flan dish. Line with foil or baking parchment and dried beans. Bake in a preheated oven at 375°F for 15 minutes. Remove the beans and foil or paper and cook for a further 10 minutes, until crisp.

3 To make the filling, beat the butter and sugar in a bowl and gradually beat in the eggs with the unsweetened cocoa. Melt the chocolate and beat it into the mixture with the light cream and the chocolate extract.

4 Pour the mixture into the cooked pie shell and bake at 325°F for 45 minutes, or until the filling is set.

5 Let cool completely, then transfer the pie to a serving plate, if desired. Cover with the whipped cream and chill.

6 To make small chocolate curls, use a peeler to remove curls from the bar of chocolate. Decorate the pie and chill.

Chocolate Fruit Tartlets

Serves 6

INGREDIENTS

1¼ cups all-purpose flour
3 tbsp unsweetened cocoa
⅔ cup butter
3 tbsp superfine sugar

2–3 tbsp water
1¾ ounces dark chocolate
½ cup chopped mixed nuts, toasted
12 ounces prepared fruit

3 tbsp apricot preserve or red
currant jelly

1 Sift together the flour and unsweetened cocoa into a mixing bowl. Cut the butter into small pieces and rub it into the flour with your fingertips until the mixture resembles fine breadcrumbs.

2 Stir in the sugar. Add just enough of the water to mix to a soft dough, approximately 1–2 tablespoons. Cover and chill in the refrigerator for about 15 minutes.

3 Roll out the dough on a lightly floured surface and use to line six 4-inch tartlet pans. Prick the dough with a fork and line the pie shells with a little crumpled foil. Bake in a preheated oven at 375°F for 10 minutes.

4 Remove the foil and bake for a further 5–10 minutes, until the pastry is crisp. Place the pans on a wire rack to cool completely.

5 Melt the chocolate. Spread out the chopped nuts on a plate. Remove the pie shells from the tins pans. Spread melted chocolate on the rims, then dip in the nuts. Let set.

6 Arrange the fruit in the tartlet shells. Melt the apricot preserve or red currant jelly with the remaining 1 tablespoon of water and brush it over the fruit. Chill the tartlets until required.

VARIATION

If desired, you can fill the cases with a little sweetened cream before topping with the fruit. For a chocolate-flavored filling, blend 8 ounces chocolate hazelnut spread with 5 tablespoons of thick yogurt or whipped cream.

Banana Cream Puffs

Serves 4–6

INGREDIENTS

CHOUX PASTRY:
²/₃ cup water
¹/₄ cup butter
³/₄ cup strong all-purpose
   flour, sifted
2 eggs

CHOCOLATE SAUCE:
3¹/₂ ounces dark chocolate, broken
   into pieces
2 tbsp water
4 tbsp confectioners' sugar
2 tbsp sweet butter

FILLING:
1¹/₄ cups heavy cream
1 banana
2 tbsp confectioners' sugar
2 tbsp banana-flavored liqueur

1 Lightly grease a cookie sheet and sprinkle with a little water. To make the pastry, place the water in a pan. Cut the butter into small pieces and add to the pan. Heat gently until the butter melts, then bring to a rolling boil. Remove the pan from the heat and add the flour all at once, beating well until the mixture leaves the sides of the pan and forms a ball. Let cool slightly, then gradually beat in the eggs to form a smooth, glossy mixture. Spoon the paste into a large pastry bag fitted with a ¹/₂-inch plain tip.

2 Pipe about 18 small balls of the paste onto the prepared cookie sheet, allowing enough room for them to expand during cooking. Bake in a preheated oven at 425°F for 15–20 minutes, until crisp and golden. Remove from the oven and make a small slit in each one for the steam to escape. Transfer to a wire rack and let cool completely.

3 To make the sauce, heat all the ingredients in a double boiler, stirring until combined to make a smooth sauce.

4 To make the filling, whip the cream until standing in soft peaks. Using a fork, mash the banana with the sugar and liqueur. Fold into the cream. Place the filling in a pastry bag fitted with a ¹/₂-inch plain tip and pipe into the cream puffs. Serve with the sauce poured on top.

Candies & Drinks

There is nothing quite as nice as home-made chocolates and sweets – they leave the average box of chocolates in the shade!

You'll find recipes in this chapter to suit everybody's taste. Wonderful, rich, melt-in-the-mouth chocolate truffles, crispy florentines, nutty chocolate creams and rich chocolate liqueurs – they're all here. There is even some simple-to-make chocolate fudge, so there is no need to fiddle about with sugar thermometers.

Looking for something to wash it all down? We have included two delightfully cool summer chocolate drinks and for warmth and comfort on winter nights two hot drinks that will simply put instant hot chocolate to shame. Enjoy!

Rocky Road Bites

Makes 18

INGREDIENTS

4¹/₂ ounces milk chocolate
2¹/₂ ounces mini multicolored
   marshmallows

¹/₄ cup chopped walnuts
1 ounce no-need-to-soak dried
   apricots, chopped

1 Line a cookie sheet with baking parchment and set aside.

2 Break the milk chocolate into small pieces and melt in a double boiler.

3 Stir in the marsh-mallows, walnuts, and apricots and toss in the melted chocolate until the ingredients are completely coated in the chocolate.

4 Place heaping teaspoons of the mixture onto the prepared cookie sheet.

5 Chill the candies in the refrigerator until they are completely set.

6 Once set, carefully remove the candies from the baking parchment.

7 The chewy bites can be placed in paper candy cases to serve, if desired.

COOK'S TIP

These candies can be stored in a cool, dry place for up to 2 weeks.

VARIATION

Light, fluffy marshmallows are available in white or pastel colors. If you cannot find mini marshmallows, use large ones and snip them into smaller pieces with kitchen scissors before mixing them into the melted chocolate in step 3.

Easy Chocolate Fudge

Makes 25–30 pieces

INGREDIENTS

1 lb 2 ounces dark chocolate	14 ounce can sweetened condensed	½ tsp vanilla extract
⅓ cup sweet butter	milk	

1 Lightly grease an 8-inch square cake pan.

2 Break the chocolate into pieces and place in a large saucepan with the butter and condensed milk.

3 Heat gently, stirring until the chocolate and butter melt and the mixture is smooth. Do not allow to boil.

4 Remove the pan from the heat. Beat in the vanilla extract, then beat the mixture for a few minutes until thickened. Pour it into the prepared pan and level the top.

5 Chill the mixture in the refrigerator until firm.

6 Tip the fudge out onto a cutting board and cut into squares to serve.

VARIATION

For chocolate peanut fudge, replace 4 tablespoons of the butter with crunchy peanut butter.

COOK'S TIP

Store the fudge in an airtight container in a cool, dry place for up to 1 month. Do not freeze.

COOK'S TIP

Don't use milk chocolate as the results will be too sticky.

No-Cook Fruit & Nut Chocolate Fudge

Makes about 25 pieces

INGREDIENTS

9 ounces dark chocolate

2 tbsp butter

4 tbsp evaporated milk

3 cups confectioners' sugar, sifted

1/2 cup roughly chopped hazelnuts

1/3 cup golden raisins

1 Lightly grease an 8-inch square cake pan.

2 Break the chocolate into pieces and melt in a double boiler with the butter and evaporated milk. Stir until the chocolate and butter have melted and the ingredients are well combined.

3 Remove from the heat and gradually beat in the confectioners' sugar. Stir the hazelnuts and golden raisins into the mixture. Press the fudge into the prepared pan and level the top. Chill until firm.

4 Tip the fudge out onto a cutting board and cut into squares. Place in paper candy cases. Chill until required.

VARIATION

Vary the nuts used in this recipe; try making the fudge with almonds, brazil nuts, walnuts, or pecans.

COOK'S TIP

The fudge can be stored in an airtight container for up to 2 weeks.

Nutty Chocolate Clusters

Makes about 30

INGREDIENTS

6 ounces white chocolate
3 1/2 ounces graham crackers
1 cup chopped macadamia nuts or
    brazil nuts

1 ounce preserved ginger,
    chopped (optional)
6 ounces dark chocolate

1 Line a cookie sheet with baking parchment. Break the white chocolate into small pieces and melt in a double boiler.

2 Break the graham crackers into small pieces. Stir the graham crackers into the melted chocolate, together with the chopped nuts and preserved ginger, if using.

3 Place heaping teaspoons of the mixture onto the prepared cookie sheet.

4 Chill the mixture in the refrigerator until set, then carefully remove the clusters from the baking parchment.

5 Melt the dark chocolate and let cool slightly. Dip the clusters into the melted chocolate, allowing the excess to drip back into the bowl. Return the clusters to the cookie sheet and chill in the refrigerator until set.

COOK'S TIP

The clusters can be stored for up to 1 week in a cool, dry place.

COOK'S TIP

Macadamia and brazil nuts are both rich-tasting and high in fat, which makes them particularly popular for confectionery, but other nuts can be used, if desired.

Chocolate Cherries

Makes 24

INGREDIENTS

12 candied cherries
2 tbsp rum or brandy

9 ounces marzipan
5 1/2 ounces dark chocolate

extra milk, dark, or white chocolate,
to decorate (optional)

1 Line a cookie sheet with baking parchment.

2 Cut the cherries in half and place them in a small bowl. Add the rum or brandy and stir to coat. Set the cherries aside to soak for a minimum of 1 hour, stirring occasionally.

3 Divide the marzipan into 24 pieces and roll each piece into a ball. Press half a marinated cherry into the top of each marzipan ball.

4 Break the chocolate into pieces and melt in a double boiler.

5 Dip each candy into the melted chocolate, allowing the excess to drip back into the pan. Place the coated cherries on the baking parchment and chill until set.

6 If desired, melt a little extra chocolate and drizzle it over the top of the coated cherries. Let set.

VARIATION

*Flatten the marzipan
and use it to mold around
the cherries to cover
them, then dip in the
chocolate as above.*

VARIATION

*Use a whole almond
in place of the halved
candied cherries and omit
the rum or brandy.*

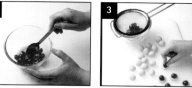

Chocolate Marzipans

Makes about 30

INGREDIENTS

1 pound marzipan
⅓ cup very finely chopped
   candied cherries

1 ounce preserved ginger, very
   finely chopped
¼ cup no-need-to-soak dried
   apricots, very finely chopped

12 ounces dark chocolate
1 ounces white chocolate
confectioners' sugar, to dust

1 Line a cookie sheet with baking parchment. Divide the marzipan into 3 balls and knead each ball to soften it.

2 Work the candied cherries into one portion of the marzipan by kneading on a surface lightly dusted with confectioners' sugar.

3 Work the preserved ginger into a second portion of marzipan, and then work the apricots into the third portion of marzipan in the same way.

4 Form each flavored portion of marzipan into small balls, making sure the flavors are kept separate.

5 Melt the dark chocolate in a double boiler. Dip one of each flavored ball of marzipan into the chocolate by spiking each one with a toothpick, allowing the excess chocolate to drip back into the pan.

6 Carefully place the balls in clusters of the three flavors on the prepared cookie sheet. Repeat with the remaining marzipan balls. Chill until set.

7 Melt the white chocolate and drizzle a little over the tops of each cluster of marzipan balls. Chill until hardened, then remove from the baking parchment and dust with sugar to serve.

VARIATION

Coat the marzipan balls in white or milk chocolate and drizzle with dark chocolate, if desired.

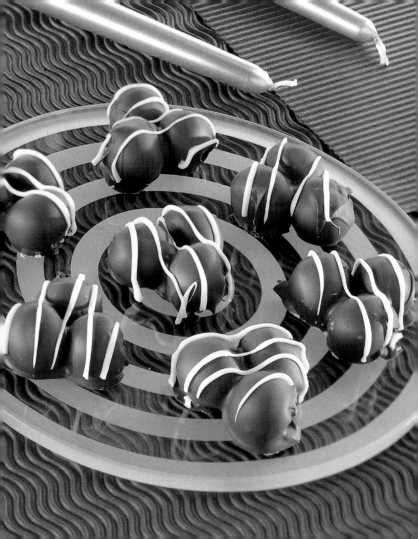

Chocolate Liqueurs

Makes 20

INGREDIENTS

3½ ounces dark chocolate
about 5 candied cherries, halved
about 10 hazelnuts or
    macadamia nuts
⅔ cup heavy cream
2 tbsp confectioners' sugar
4 tbsp liqueur

TO FINISH:
1¾ ounces dark chocolate, melted
a little white chocolate, melted,
    or white chocolate curls
    (see page 66), or extra nuts
    and cherries

1 Line a cookie sheet with baking parchment. Melt the chocolate and spoon it into 20 paper candy cases, spreading up the sides with a small spoon or pastry brush. Place upside down on the prepared cookie sheet and let set.

2 Carefully peel away the paper cases. Place a cherry or nut in the base of each cup.

3 To make the filling, place the heavy cream in a mixing bowl and sift the confectioners' sugar on top. Whip the cream until it is just holding its shape, then beat in the liqueur.

4 Place the cream in a pastry bag fitted with a ½-inch plain tip and pipe a little into each chocolate case. Set aside in the refrigerator to chill for 20 minutes.

5 To finish, spoon the melted dark chocolate over the cream to cover it, and pipe the melted white chocolate on top, swirling it into the dark chocolate with a toothpick. Set aside to harden. Alternatively, cover the cream with the melted dark chocolate and decorate with white chocolate curls before setting. Or, place a small piece of nut or cherry on top of the cream and then cover with dark chocolate.

COOK'S TIP

Candy cases can vary in size. Use the smallest you can find for this recipe.

Chocolate Cups with Mascarpone Filling

Makes 20

INGREDIENTS

3¹/₂ ounces dark chocolate	FILLING: 3¹/₂ ounces milk or dark chocolate ¹/₄ tsp vanilla extract	1 cup mascarpone cheese unsweetened cocoa, to dust

1 Line a cookie sheet with baking parchment. Melt the chocolate and spoon it into 20 paper candy cases, spreading up the sides with a small spoon or pastry brush. Place upside down on the prepared cookie sheet and let set.

2 When set, carefully peel away the paper cases.

3 To make the filling, melt the dark or milk chocolate. Place the mascarpone cheese in a bowl, beat in the vanilla extract and melted chocolate, and beat until well combined.

Chill the mixture in the refrigerator, beating occasionally until firm enough to pipe.

4 Place the mascarpone filling in a pastry bag fitted with a star tip and pipe the mixture into the cups. Decorate with a dusting of unsweetened cocoa.

COOK'S TIP

Mascarpone is a rich Italian soft cheese made from fresh cream, so it has a high fat content. Its delicate flavor blends well with chocolate.

VARIATION

You can use lightly whipped heavy cream instead of the mascarpone cheese, if desired.

Mini Chocolate Cones

Makes 10

INGREDIENTS

2³/₄ ounces dark chocolate
¹/₃ cup heavy cream

1 tbsp confectioners' sugar
1 tbsp crème de menthe

chocolate coffee beans, to
decorate (optional)

1 Cut ten 3-inch rounds of baking parchment. Shape each round into a cone shape and secure with tape.

2 Melt the chocolate. Using a small pastry brush or clean artists' brush, brush the inside of each cone with melted chocolate.

3 Brush a second layer of chocolate on the inside of the cones and chill until set. Carefully peel away the paper.

4 Place the heavy cream, confectioners' sugar, and crème de menthe in a

mixing bowl and whip until just holding its shape. Place in a pastry bag fitted with a star tip and pipe the mixture into the chocolate cones.

5 Decorate the cones with chocolate coffee beans (if using) and chill in the refrigerator until required.

COOK'S TIP

The chocolate cones can be made in advance and kept in the refrigerator for up to 1 week. Do not fill them more than 2 hours before you are going to serve them.

VARIATION

Use a different flavored liqueur to flavor the cream: a coffee-flavored liqueur is perfect. If you want a mint flavor without using a liqueur, use a few drops of peppermint extract to flavor the cream, according to taste.

Collettes

Makes 20

INGREDIENTS

3$\frac{1}{2}$ ounces white chocolate	FILLING: 5$\frac{1}{2}$ ounces orange-flavored dark chocolate	$\frac{2}{3}$ cup heavy cream 2 tbsp confectioners' sugar

1 Line a cookie sheet with baking parchment. Melt the chocolate and spoon it into 20 paper candy cases, spreading up the sides with a small spoon or pastry brush. Place upside down on the prepared cookie sheet and let set.

2 When set, carefully peel away the paper cases.

3 To make the filling, melt the orange-flavored chocolate and place in a mixing bowl with the heavy cream and the confectioners' sugar. Beat until smooth. Chill in the refrigerator, stirring occasionally, until the mixture becomes firm enough to pipe.

4 Place the filling in a pastry bag fitted with a star tip and pipe a little into each case. Chill in the refrigerator until required.

VARIATION

Add 1 tbsp orange-flavored liqueur to the filling, if desired.

COOK'S TIP

If they do not hold their shape well, use 2 cases to make a double thickness mold. Foil cases are firmer, so use these if desired.

Use the smallest candy cases you can find for these cups.

Mini Florentines

Makes about 40

INGREDIENTS

1/3 cup butter
1/3 cup superfine sugar
2 tbsp golden raisins

2 tbsp chopped candied cherries
2 tbsp candied ginger, chopped
1/4 cup sunflower seeds

3/4 cup slivered almonds
2 tbsp heavy cream
6 ounces dark or milk chocolate

1 Lightly grease and flour 2 cookie sheets or line with baking parchment. Place the butter in a small pan and heat gently until melted. Add the sugar, stir until dissolved, then bring the mixture to a boil. Remove from the heat and stir in the golden raisins, cherries, ginger, sunflower seeds, and almonds. Mix well, then beat in the cream.

2 Place small teaspoons of the fruit and nut mixture onto the prepared cookie sheets, allowing plenty of space for the mixture to spread. Bake in a preheated oven at 350°F for 10–12 minutes, until light golden in color.

3 Remove from the oven and, while still hot, use a circular cookie cutter to pull in the edges to form a perfect round. Let cool and crispen before removing from the cookie sheet.

4 Melt most of the chocolate and spread it on a sheet of baking parchment. When the chocolate is on the point of setting, place the cookies, flat side down, on the chocolate and allow to harden completely.

5 Cut around the florentines and remove from the paper. Spread a little more chocolate on the already coated side of the florentines and use a fork to mark waves in the chocolate. Let set. Arrange the florentines on a plate (or in a presentation box for a gift), with alternate sides facing upward. Keep cool.

Mini Chocolate Tartlets

Makes about 18

INGREDIENTS

1¹/₂ cups all-purpose flour
¹/₃ cup butter
1 tbsp superfine sugar
about 1 tbsp water

FILLING:
¹/₂ cup cream cheese
5 tsp superfine sugar
1 small egg, lightly beaten
1³/₄ ounces dark chocolate

TO DECORATE:
¹/₃ cup heavy cream
dark chocolate curls (see page 214)
unsweetened cocoa, to dust

1 Sift the flour into a mixing bowl. Cut the butter into small pieces and rub it in with your fingertips until the mixture resembles fine breadcrumbs. Stir in the sugar. Add just enough water to mix to a soft dough, then cover, and chill in the refrigerator for 15 minutes.

2 Roll out the pie dough on a lightly floured surface and use to line 18 mini tartlet pans or mini muffin pans. Prick the bases with a toothpick.

3 Beat together the cream cheese and the sugar until smooth. Beat in the egg. Melt the chocolate and beat it into the mixture. Spoon into the pie shells and bake in a preheated oven at 375°F for about 15 minutes, until the pastry is crisp and the filling set. Place the pans on a wire rack to cool completely.

4 Chill the tartlets in the refrigerator. Whip the cream until it is just holding its shape. Place in a pastry bag fitted with a star tip. Pipe rosettes of cream on top of the tartlets. Decorate with chocolate curls and dust with unsweetened cocoa.

COOK'S TIP

The tartlets can be made up to 3 days ahead. Decorate on the day of serving, preferably no more than 4 hours in advance.

Rum Truffles

Makes about 20

INGREDIENTS

5¹/₂ ounces dark chocolate
small pat of butter
2 tbsp rum

¹/₂ cup shredded coconut
2 cups cake crumbs

6 tbsp confectioners' sugar
2 tbsp unsweetened cocoa

1 Break the chocolate into pieces and melt with the butter in a double boiler.

2 Remove the melted chocolate from the heat and beat in the rum. Stir in the shredded coconut, cake crumbs, and 4 tablespoons of the confectioners' sugar. Beat until well combined. Add a little extra rum if the mixture is too stiff.

3 Roll the mixture into small, evenly-sized balls and place them on a sheet of baking parchment. Chill in the refrigerator until firm.

4 Sift the remaining confectioners' sugar onto a large plate. Sift the unsweetened cocoa onto another plate. Roll half of the truffles in the confectioners' sugar until coated, and roll the remaining truffles in the unsweetened cocoa.

5 Place the truffles in paper candy cases and chill in the refrigerator until required.

VARIATION

Make the truffles with white chocolate and replace the rum with coconut liqueur or milk, if desired. Roll them in unsweetened cocoa or dip in melted milk chocolate.

COOK'S TIP

These truffles will keep for about 2 weeks in a cool place.

White Chocolate Truffles

Makes about 20

INGREDIENTS

2 tbsp sweet butter
5 tbsp heavy cream
8 ounces good quality Swiss
   white chocolate

1 tbsp orange-flavored liqueur
(optional)

TO FINISH:
3¹/₂ ounces white chocolate

1 Line a jelly roll pan with baking parchment.

2 Place the butter and cream in a small saucepan and bring slowly to a boil, stirring constantly. Boil for 1 minute, then remove from the heat.

3 Break the chocolate into pieces and add to the cream. Stir until melted, then beat in the liqueur, if using.

4 Pour into the prepared pan and chill for about 2 hours until firm.

5 Break off pieces of mixture and roll them into balls. Chill for a further 30 minutes before finishing the truffles.

6 To finish, melt the white chocolate. Dip the balls in the chocolate, allowing the excess to drip back into the bowl. Place on nonstick baking parchment and swirl the chocolate with a fork. Let harden.

7 Drizzle a little melted dark chocolate over the truffles if desired and let set. Place the truffles in paper cases to serve.

COOK'S TIP

The truffle mixture needs to be firm, but not too hard to roll. If the mixture is too hard, allow it to stand at room temperature for a few minutes to soften slightly. During rolling the mixture will become sticky but will re-harden in the refrigerator before coating.

COOK'S TIP

The chocolates can be kept in the refrigerator for up to 2 weeks.

Italian Chocolate Truffles

Makes about 24

INGREDIENTS

6 ounces dark chocolate

2 tbsp almond-flavored
liqueur (amaretto) or orange-
flavored liqueur

3 tbsp sweet butter

$^1/_2$ cup confectioners' sugar

$^1/_2$ cup ground almonds

$1^3/_4$ ounces grated chocolate

1 Melt the dark chocolate with the liqueur in a double boiler, stirring until well combined.

2 Add the butter and stir until it has melted. Stir in the confectioners' sugar and the ground almonds.

3 Leave the mixture in a cool place until firm enough to roll into about 24 balls.

4 Place the grated chocolate on a plate and roll the truffles in the chocolate to coat them.

5 Place the truffles in paper candy cases and chill.

COOK'S TIP

These truffles will keep for about 2 weeks in a cool place.

VARIATION

The almond-flavored liqueur gives these truffles an authentic Italian flavor. The original almond liqueur, Amaretto di Saronno, comes from Saronno in Italy.

VARIATION

For a sweeter truffle, use milk chocolate instead of dark. Dip the truffles in melted chocolate to finish, if desired.

Hot Chocolate Drinks

Serves 2

INGREDIENTS

SPICY HOT CHOCOLATE:
2¹/₂ cups milk
1 tsp apple pie spice
3¹/₂ ounces dark chocolate
4 cinnamon sticks
¹/₃ cup heavy cream, lightly
    whipped

HOT CHOCOLATE & ORANGE TODDY:
2¹/₂ ounces orange-flavored
    dark chocolate
2¹/₂ cups milk
3 tbsp rum
2 tbsp heavy cream
grated nutmeg

1 To make Spicy Hot Chocolate, pour the milk into a small pan. Sprinkle the apple pie spice into the pan.

2 Break the dark chocolate into squares and add to the milk. Heat the mixture over a low heat until the milk is just boiling, stirring all the time to prevent the milk from burning on the bottom of the pan.

3 Place 2 cinnamon sticks in 2 cups and pour in the spicy hot chocolate. Top with the whipped heavy cream and serve immediately.

4 To make Hot Chocolate & Orange Toddy, break the orange-flavored dark chocolate into squares and place in a small saucepan with the milk. Heat over a low heat until just boiling, stirring constantly.

5 Remove the pan from the heat and stir in the rum. Pour into cups.

6 Pour the cream over the back of a spoon or swirl onto the top so that it sits on top of the hot chocolate. Sprinkle with grated nutmeg and serve at once.

COOK'S TIP

Using a cinnamon stick as a stirrer will give any hot chocolate drink a sweet, pungent flavor of cinnamon, without overpowering the flavor of the chocolate.

Cold Chocolate Drinks

Serves 2

| INGREDIENTS |

CHOCOLATE MILK SHAKE:
2 cups ice-cold milk
3 tbsp drinking chocolate powder

3 scoops chocolate ice cream
unsweetened cocoa powder, to dust
(optional)

CHOCOLATE ICE CREAM SODA:
5 tbsp chocolate dessert sauce
soda water
2 scoops chocolate ice cream
heavy cream, whipped
dark or milk chocolate, grated

1 To make Chocolate Milk Shake, place half the ice-cold milk in a blender.

2 Add the chocolate powder to the blender and 1 scoop of the chocolate ice cream. Blend until the mixture is frothy and well mixed. Stir in the remaining milk.

3 Place the remaining 2 scoops of chocolate ice cream in 2 serving glasses and carefully pour the chocolate milk over the ice cream.

4 Sprinkle a little unsweetened cocoa (if using) over the top of each drink and serve at once.

5 To make Chocolate Ice Cream Soda, divide the chocolate dessert sauce between 2 glasses. (You can use a ready-made chocolate dessert sauce, or the hot chocolate sauce on page 160, or the glossy chocolate sauce on page 188.)

6 Add a little soda water to each glass and stir to combine the sauce and soda water. Place a scoop of ice cream in each glass and top up with more soda water.

7 Place a large spoon of whipped cream on the top, if desired, and sprinkle with a little grated dark or milk chocolate.

COOK'S TIP

Served in a tall glass, a milk shake or an ice cream soda makes a scrumptious snack in a drink. Serve with straws, if wished.

Index

Index compiled by Hilary Bird